Hearing Film

Tracking Identifications in Contemporary Hollywood Film Music

Anahid Kassabian

Routledge
NEW YORK AND LONDON

Published in 2001 by
Routledge
29 West 35th Street
New York, NY 10001

Published in Great Britain by
Routledge
11 New Fetter Lane
London EC4P 4EE

Copyright © 2001 by Routledge
An imprint of the Taylor & Francis Group

Printed in the United States of America on acid-free paper.
Design and typography: Jack Donner

Library of Congress Cataloging-in-Publication Data

Kassabian, Anahid.
    Hearing film : tracking identifications in contemporary Hollywood film music /
      Anahid Kassabian
      p.   cm.
    Includes bibliographical references and indexes.
    ISBN 0–415–92853–2 — ISBN 0–415–92854–0 (pbk.)
      1. Motion picture music—United States—History and criticism. 2. Motion
pictures and music. I. Title.
    ML2075 .K39 2000
    781.5'42—dc21   00–044636

Contents

Acknowledgments

Incomplete though these thanks are, they go to:

The ones who hung in from beginning to end: Iris Kassabian, Elizabeth Kazanjian, Patricia Clough. And the ones who read drafts—sometimes many—much to the benefit of the final product: Shaleen Brawn, Alex Chasin, Simon Frith, Regenia Gagnier, Barbara Gelpi, Miranda Joseph, David Kazanjian, Kelly Mays, Amit Rai, David Schwarz, Ola Stockfelt, Philip Tagg, and the anonymous readers of both articles and the final book.

The organization: the International Association for the Study of Popular Music, which always welcomed this work, and whose members helped me refine it over the years. The institutions that financed and supported the research: Fordham University; Stanford University; the Kaltenborn Foundation; the American-Scandinavian Foundation; Musikvetenskapliga Institutionen, Göteborgs Universitet; the Whiting Foundation.

The researchers: John Acquaviva, Prudence Hill, Jane Mc-Gonigal, and Jennifer Weeks, who found images, permissions, box office receipts, and typos with amazing charm and alacrity. The music magicians: David Gottlieb and Robert Bowen, who transcribed and/or checked, then typeset, every music example in this book.

The ones who intervened at crucial moments: Soo Mee Kwon, Routledge's former music editor, and disability specialists Sandy

Cohen, Fern Geschwind, Ray Grott, George Symkiewicz, Bob Tellería, and Monica Worline.

The many friends and colleagues, too numerous to list, who encouraged me and held my hand at various stages, including: Robin Andersen, David Brackett, Paul Chan, Norman Cowie, Nicole Fermon, Linda Garber, Reebee Garofalo, Larry Grossberg, Lisa Hogeland, Gwenyth Jackaway, Steve Jones, Mary Klages, Eline Maxwell, Leerom Medovoi, Monica Moore, Sue Pavy, Brian Rose, Josefina Saldaña, Dave Sanjek, Eva Stadler, Elizabeth Stone, and Scott Walker.

And, most importantly, the partners: Leo G. Svendsen and Maral Kassabian Svendsen. Without you, no book would matter.

Portions of chapter 4 appeared in *Studies in Symbolic Interaction*, vol. 15, Norman Denzin, ed. (Greenwich, CT: JAI Press, 1994).

Portions of chapter 5 appeared in *Keeping Score: Music, Disciplinarity, Culture*, Schwarz, Kassabian, and Siegel, eds. (Charlottesville, VA: University Press of Virginia, 1997).

Parts of this manuscript were written with Dragon Dictate and Dragon Naturally Speaking voice-recognition programs. My thanks to Dragon Systems and its programmers for making writing possible for so many of us.

Hearing Film

Listening for Identifications
A Prologue

I can hear it as if it were yesterday. I was sitting in a classroom, "watching" John Cassavetes's *A Woman Under the Influence*. My heart broke every time I heard Gena Rowlands sing the "Dying Swan," and my eyes welled with tears at the image of a black laborer singing "Celeste Aïda" for a dozen of his coworkers at the breakfast table of this tortured, crazy Italian-American lady. Why, I wondered, did none of the course readings, and none of the readings in any other courses, care about or try to explain this experience? Why didn't they attend to film's music, when it seemed to me so obviously crucial? I spent my senior year, and my first year or two in graduate school in the mid-eighties, writing about that film and its music. (My friends referred to it as the only film I'd ever seen.) Fifteen years later, it hardly appears in this book; my questions eventually drew me elsewhere. But its shadows are throughout.

Hearing Film begins from a simple premise I first began to think about in class that day. Music draws filmgoers into a film's world, measure by measure. It is, I will argue, at least as significant as the visual and narrative components that have dominated film studies. It conditions identification processes, the encounters between film texts and filmgoers' psyches. The study of film music, however, cannot begin by simply tagging music on to previous approaches to film.

Hearing Film calls for a major shift in the study of film. First, any story of identifications with films must take account of engagements between filmgoers and film scores. Second, those engagements are conditioned by filmgoers' relationships to a wide range of musics both within and outside of their filmgoing practices. Third, the study of film music both requires and enables the study of the political and social relations of contemporary life.

Identification processes through film music cannot be understood in a single way—not all scores offer similar paths to identifications. There are two main approaches to film music in contemporary Hollywood: the composed score, a body of musical material composed specifically for the film in question; and the compiled score, a score built of songs that often (but not always) preexisted the film. Composed scores, most often associated with classical Hollywood scoring traditions, condition what I call *assimilating identifications*. Such paths are structured to draw perceivers[1] into socially and historically unfamiliar positions, as do larger scale processes of assimilation.

When an offer of assimilating identification is (unconsciously) accepted, perceivers can easily find themselves positioned anywhere—sledding down the Himalayas, for instance—and with anyone—a Lithuanian sub captain, perhaps, or a swashbuckling Mexican orphan peasant.[2] There is no necessary relationship between film perceivers and the identity positions they take on in an assimilating identification. Nor is there any relationship between their own histories and the positions. Scores that offer assimilating identifications, I argue, try to maintain fairly rigid control over such processes, even as—or because—they encourage unlikely identifications.

Compiled scores, however, can operate quite differently. With their range of complete songs used just as they are heard on the radio, they bring the immediate threat of history. Most people in the movie theater, even on opening day, have probably heard at least a few of the songs before, whether the score is made up of oldies or new releases. Airplay for the songs may serve as good advertising for the film, but it means that perceivers bring external associations with the songs into their engagements with the film.[3] A score that offers assimilating identifications is much harder to construct from such songs. More often, compiled scores offer what I call *affiliating identifications*, and they operate quite differently from composed scores. These ties depend on histories forged outside the film scene, and they allow for a fair bit of mobility within it. If offers of assimilating identifications try to narrow the psychic field, then offers of affiliating identifications open it wide. This difference is, to my mind, at the heart of filmgoers' relationships to contemporary film music.

I chose to focus on contemporary films for several reasons. First, we have heard a great flowering in film music. The thick expansive orchestral scores of John Williams and Danny Elfman have been side-by-side in theaters with, on the one hand, the much sparer sounds of Hans Zimmer and Terence Blanchard, and on the other with compiled scores of music by Sublime, Celine Dion, Dinah Washington, Barrio Boyz, Marianne Faithfull, Los Fabulosos Cadillacs, Nusrat Fateh Ali Khan, and Pinetop Perkins. The soundtracks of the 1980s and 1990s provide a veritable candy store for film music scholars.

Second, there is far too little work in this area. Film music scholarship has privileged mass-market U.S. films of the first half of the twentieth century, from silents to "classical Hollywood."[4] Substantial work has been done on silent film music (Anderson 1987; Marks 1997), where questions focus on sources of musical materials and performance practices. Most film music scholarship focuses heavily, if not exclusively, on classical Hollywood practices (Gorbman 1987; Flinn 1992; Kalinak 1992; and Brown 1994). In this scholarship, the concerns have been dominated by the music's relationship to the film's narrative systems and operations.

Third, contemporary films pose a new set of problems to film music scholars. First, decades of political struggles by women and people of color have made possible films—*Mississippi Masala, Mi Familia/My Family, Thelma and Louise, Mi Vida Loca, Boyz N the Hood, Waiting to Exhale,* and *Malcolm X*—that would never have been made under the classical Hollywood studio system. These films have not only changed the narrative landscape of mainstream moviemaking, but they have also significantly broadened its range of musical materials.

Fourth, I have chosen to work on contemporary Hollywood film because I find some versions of the return to historicism in film studies disturbing. "The end result has been a new antiquarianism, [which] seeks to delegitimize the sort of engaged interventionist analysis that made film theory such a vital force in the academy during the 1970s and 1980s" (Collins, Radner, and Collins 1993: 2–3). My focus on the 1980s and 1990s allows me to consider film music's role in the changing pressures of identity formations such as race, ethnicity, sexuality, and gender.

Finally, the pandering of mass media industries first to the "baby boom generation" and more recently to "Gen X" has led to an explosion in the use of compiled soundtracks. These soundtracks pose an entire new field of questions for film music scholars. For example, Jeff Smith (1998) discusses the placement and marketing of songs in such scores. Daniel Goldmark suggested recently that there are important questions about the gendered division of labor and the roles of composers versus music supervisors, the people (often women) who choose the music for compiled scores.[5] My argument here is a comparative one: compiled scores offer

affiliating identifications, a major shift from the assimilating identifications offered by classical Hollywood scoring practices.

This book treats contemporary film music because it is an
understudied arena that provides an occasion to think through
new musical materials, composition practices, narrative land-
scapes, psychic processes, and social contexts.

Over the course of film's century-long existence, film music has
always had an odd status. On the one hand, it has been a subject
of much discussion. There is an enormous body of public intellectual, journalistic criticism, in the form of reviews of scores and
recordings and interviews with and biographies of great composers. There is also a slimmer body of scholarly work, from early
works like Kurt London's 1936 *Film Music* to Royal S. Brown's 1994
Overtones and Undertones. On the other hand, no significant body of
criticism actively includes analysis of film music; it has rarely been
pursued by the semiotic, narratological, or psychoanalytic theorists of (what they call) "film." The film of these theorists and
their theories, seen but never heard, was more silent than any
silent film. So not only has film music scholarship failed to ignite
broad swaths of critical imagination, but the music itself has, for
the most part, been bracketed from film scholarship altogether.

Hearing Film seeks, quite bluntly, to change all that. There is no
more sense in calling a visual object of analysis a "film" than there
is in calling a screenplay a "film." A film as perceived by any kind
of audience—public or scholarly—has words, sounds, images,
and music. It is not merely *seen*, as in "I saw the greatest film the
other day," nor simply viewed by "film viewers." Music and filmgoers engage each other in bonds that intersect other tracks of
films in complicated ways. My purpose, here, is to help provide
some tools for considering both the identifications and the role of
those ties in perceivers' experiences of films.

Like all forms of culture, music presents its students with particular problems. One argument, for example, suggests that music is somehow specifically and unmediatedly of the body, that music works on listeners at least in part without the mediation of culture. Some music scholars argue that rhythm, volume, and vocal timbre are acoustical relations between physics (e.g., sound wave characteristics) and physiology (e.g., increased pulse rate).[6] This is undeniable, as are the relations between physics and physiology that condition vision; the very perception of motion on film relies on them. This is no site on which to distinguish music from verbal or visual representations.

The significant difference between words or pictures and music is, rather, that music is *understood* as nonrepresentational. The heated nineteenth-century debates about program music attest to the commitment of many musicians and composers to this notion. Certainly, most of twentieth-century western art music composition styles—atonality, serialism, aleatory music, computer compositional procedures, and perhaps even minimalism—depend on the notion that music does not "mean" in any direct sense of the term. But the word shift within this paragraph is precisely the shift that takes place in debates over meaning and music: somehow, "representation" and "meaning" come to be synonymous, and arguments that music is "nonrepresentational" are (implicitly, at least) understood as proving that music does not "mean" in any recognizable sense of the term.

I contest this notion quite strongly, for several reasons. First, considerations of music "in general" seem inevitably to take post-Enlightenment western art music as their point of departure (see, e.g., Kivy 1990, 1993). This logic is fascinatingly tautological: in order to consider a general question about universal properties of the organized patterns of sound that constitute music most inclusively defined, these music theorists and philosophers go directly to the music with which they are most familiar and that was produced within the epistemological framework that conditions their own thinking. Rather than considering, for example, early-nineteenth-century American whaling songs or classical Arabic improvisational music, arguments about the "absoluteness" of music depend on music written as "absolute music" to begin with.[7] Film music, while born out of the traditions of nineteenth-century European symphonic music, was never meant to be absolute; it has always been considered a meaning-making system by its producers.

Second, there is now a body of work that contests even western art music's relationship to the production of meaning. Susan McClary has argued that music is ideologically marked:

> ... the Mozart piano concerto movement with which we are concerned neither makes up its own rules nor derives them from some abstract, absolute, transcendental source. Rather it depends heavily on conventions of eighteenth-century harmonic syntax, formal procedure, genre type, rhythmic propriety, gestural vocabulary, and associations. All of these conventions have histories: social histories marked with national, economic, class and gender—that is, political—interests. (1986: 53)

That perspective on music is growing throughout the discipline. A number of books and anthologies are considering the relationships between various musics, including western art music, and other important axes of contemporary cultural analysis (e.g., gender, autonomous art, disciplinarity, sexuality, value).[8] This body of scholarship would strongly suggest that film music engages its listeners in important processes of producing and reproducing meanings and ideologies.

Third, mainstream Hollywood film music practices may well

constitute the only musical lingua franca in contemporary western industrialized societies. Because of the monopoly practices of U.S. studios in the global film, television, and music industries, virtually everyone grows into some degree of competence in the languages of film, television, and popular music. As George Antheil said,

> Your musical tastes become molded by these scores, heard without knowing it. You *see* love, and you *hear* it. Simultaneously. It makes sense. Music suddenly becomes a language for you, without your knowing it. (1945, as quoted in Thomas 1973: 171)

Rather than presenting an abstract universalism like absolute music, film music functions as a global culture that begs to be studied.

Fourth, specific musics engage with their listeners in specific modes of meaning production. While it may be the case that societies universally produce organizations of sound, it is by no means clear that everyone does so for the same or even related reasons. Music consumption in contemporary western industrialized societies is broadly figured as a leisure activity (although music is also ubiquitously present in workplaces, on telephones, and in stores). But "listening" as an act of consumption does not translate across all cultural borders; in some cultures that do not share production/consumption distinctions with advanced capitalism, music is understood as a participatory process. Even within U.S. mass-mediated musical culture, there is no reason to believe that "new country," "hip-hop," "alternative," and "classic rock" condition meaning production identically or even similarly. Different musics are meant to be listened to differently, and they engage listeners differently.

Finally, meaning production and identification processes are inextricably intertwined, and therefore any consideration of the question of meaning must inevitably consider the axis called variously "consumption," "reception," and "reading" in different theoretical paradigms. As de Certeau suggests,

> Many, often remarkable, works have sought to study the representations of a society, on the one hand, and its modes of behavior, on the other. Building on our knowledge of these social phenomena, it seems both possible and necessary to determine the use to which they are put by groups or individuals. For example, the analysis of the images broadcast by television (representation) and of the time spent watching television (behavior) should be complemented by a study of what the cultural consumer "makes" or "does" during this time and with these images. The same goes for the use of urban space, the products purchased in the supermarket, the stories and legends distributed by the newspapers, and so on. (1984: xii)

That "and so on," I am insisting, includes music in general and film music in particular. One important distinction, then, between this book and recent studies of film music is precisely this question of use. While both Gorbman (1987) and Kalinak (1992) focus in particular on the textual strategies of classical Hollywood film scores, I emphasize what de Certeau calls "use" and what I have been calling the production of meaning and processes of identification.

I have chosen to avoid the technical language of music studies wherever possible. This is not because, like some popular music scholars, I question its usefulness, but rather, because it would oppose one of my main purposes. Because music has been claimed by an expert discourse, people feel unauthorized to talk about it. Further, as Kalinak has pointed out, music has long been understood as having unmediated access to the soul (it "soothes the savage breast"), which also means that it is an article of faith that music cannot be consciously apprehended except through its expert formalist discourse.

Most people imagine that they cannot say anything about music, in spite of regular practices of buying, listening to, and often producing music. They imagine this in spite of regular conversations about songs, performers, albums, radio stations, and concerts; about what tapes they use to work out to, walk to, or cook to; about stylistic pedigrees and generic histories, and much more. While film scholars do not generally feel a need to professionalize themselves in art history or linguistics before talking about "a film," the strong hold of the "expert discourse ideology" of music has kept a tight lid on the production of studies of film music, and an even tighter lid on their routine inclusion in courses, theorizing, and criticism. I have charted a different path, one that should enable film scholars to talk about music comfortably and willingly as a routine part of their work.

To this end, there are transcriptions of musical examples throughout the book. These are piano reductions, and in no way offer themselves as objects of study to musicologists or music theorists. They are utterly insufficient to that task. But for those readers who were put through a few years of piano lessons, they offer an opportunity to hear a melodic, harmonic, and rhythmic sketch of the music under discussion. I hope sitting down and plunking them out will offer a small pleasure as well as add some support to my arguments.

Hearing Film has two main sections. The first, consisting of chapters 1 and 2, lays the groundwork for studying film music and identification processes. It provides basic tools for reading film scores from the perspective of film perceivers, tools that will be put to use in the later, analytical chapters.

The first chapter, "How Film Music Works," discusses music and ideology. Over their long history, debates about music and meaning have tended to consider music in the most general terms. I argue instead that, music in general aside, classical Hollywood film music must be thought of as a semiotic system. Musical discourse analysis raises particular problems, however, with a simple transferal of ideas about language to music. Through an analysis of a quantitative study of the responses of six hundred listeners to ten film and television title themes, I argue that film music is, for example, a gendered discourse. (The results of the study suggest that similar arguments could be made about race, sexuality, class, and their mutual imbrication.)

In the second chapter, "How Music Works in Film," I describe the relationships among single events of music and other aspects of the film. Any one instance of music has various relationships:

- to other music, both within the same film and more generally;
- to the narrative and the world it creates; and
- to other tracks of the film (visual images, dialogue, sound effects).

The purpose of this chapter is both to describe these relationships and their place in the Hollywood film music signifying system and to begin developing some vocabulary for describing them from the perspective of film perceivers. No critical or theoretical practice can proceed without such a vocabulary.

The second section of the book, chapters 3, 4, and 5, considers groups or pairs of films that raise particular questions for the study of contemporary Hollywood scores and how they condition assimilating and affiliating identification processes. Each chapter intertwines discussions of scholarship, readings of film scores, and development of a theoretical position.

"A Woman Scored" (chapter 3) considers early debates in feminist psychoanalytic film theory and in popular music studies
specifically as they bear on developing a theory of film music. I
argue that, beginning in these formative moments, each field
represses the central categories of the other. "Desire" and
"agency," concepts central to these debates, so often bubble to the
surface in both the theoretical texts of each field and the scores of
contemporary Hollywood films that they cannot be avoided. I
focus in particular on a group of films—*Dangerous Liaisons, Desert
Hearts, Bagdad Cafe, Dirty Dancing*, and *Thelma and Louise*—that put
strong female characters, desiring subjects with plenty of agency,
at their centers. After readings of both theoretical texts and films,
the chapter concludes by positing a theoretical framework particularly directed toward considering modes of identification
through music in films.

In the fourth chapter, "At the Twilight's Last Scoring," I pose the
question: What metaphors or models of identification can describe
relations of different axes of identity (e.g., gender, race, sexuality)
and different modes of textuality (visual, verbal, musical)? As part
of the liberal discourse of the nation, the category of "American"
claims to include all axes of identity. As part of the mass culture discourse of Hollywood, however, "American" is established nega-
tively precisely as excluding those identities the nation's liberal
discourse claims to include. Through critiques of three 1980s
action-adventure blockbusters (*The Hunt for Red October, Lethal Weapon
2*, and *Indiana Jones and the Temple of Doom*), I develop a theory based
on the notion of "assimilation." Subjects marginalized by dominant ideologies are not excluded in these films, but rather are
"invited" to identify temporarily with the straight white male hero,
whether or not they also manage the difficult process of identifying with a non-straight, non-white, and/or non-male character.

In the final chapter, "Opening Scores," I return to films that, like those in chapter 3, make available a wider range of identificatory possibilities. Comparing two films set in high schools—*Dangerous Minds* and *The Substitute*—and two interracial romances—*Mississippi Masala* and *Corrina, Corrina*—I consider how film scores can group together several different entry points of identification. To describe engagements with such scores, I use the metaphor of "affiliating" identifications, in contrast to the narrowing track offered for assimilating identifications. The chapter closes with a discussion of the relationships between these two directions and their relationships with and coexistence in scores.

Throughout the literature on how films engage viewers (or spectators or audiences) in identification processes, there is very little mention of music. And throughout the literature on film music, there is very little work on identification processes. Yet music is one of the major tools Hollywood films use to track identifications. Through two distinct models of contemporary Hollywood musical practice, two paths of engagement have developed. The ties between assimilating identifications and composed scores on the one hand, and affiliating identifications and compiled scores on the other, are not absolute, but they are important. Moreover, some scores combine both kinds of music and both kinds of offers of identification. There is, I hope and assume, much more to say about these questions than can be said in one book.

Hearing Film will have succeeded if you, the reader, come away convinced of three things. First, music conditions perceivers' psychic engagements with films. Second, no serious theory of identification processes can be silent. And third, different scores condition different identification processes. Weighty cultural, ideological, subjective work is done by controlling, assimilating identifications on the one hand, and by opening, affiliating ones on the other.

We make our lives in identifications with the texts around us every day. Many of these texts are music, yet we continue to think of them as background, perhaps absent from consciousness, perhaps entertaining, perhaps annoying, but in all cases ultimately innocuous. *Hearing Film* offers a different perspective on one arena of these ubiquitous sounds. It is my most dearly held hope that readers will come away from this book convinced of the importance of listening critically to films. Not as an addendum to careful visual or narrative analysis, but as a central part of any and every film critical practice. Every discourse, from political rhetoric to academic discipline-speak to fashion, demands careful, thoughtful, informed attention, and ubiquitous musics such as film music are no exception.

But the beginning of any critical practice must be a consideration of how meaning is made, the question to which I turn in the following chapter.

1

How Film Music Works

There has been a tendency in European and American thought since the Enlightenment to categorize music as a particularly pure art. Music has been understood to produce meaning only on the most abstract, spiritual, or formal levels. Baroque and pre-Baroque notions that, for example, specific scales or phrases might have specific meanings have been denounced since the Enlightenment. Music became the foremost example of autonomous art, art for art's sake. Communication of meaning came to be considered outside the realm of music's tasks; western instrumental art music is called "absolute." As Stravinsky put it:

> . . . I consider that music is, by its very nature, powerless to express anything at all, whether a feeling, an attitude of mind, a psychological mood, a phenomenon of nature. If, as is nearly always the case, music appears to express something, this is only an illusion and not a reality. (1936: 91)

Expressing the same view, Adorno argues in his typology of musical listeners that music listening ought to be concerned with form, not imagined meaning. The fourth type of listener in his hierarchy is the "emotional listener," about whom he says:

The type extends from those whom music, of whichever kind, will stimulate to visual notions and associations to men whose musical experiences approach the torpor of vague reveries.... At times such people may use music as a vessel into which they put their own anguished and, according to psychoanalytical theory, "free-flowing" emotions; at other times they will identify with the music, drawing from it the emotions they miss in themselves. (1988: 9)

And for one last example—film composer Irwin Bazelon states definitively that:

the language of music expresses only musical aesthetics: ... in its pure and absolute state [music] does not describe anything.... [T]he images it seems to conjure up in the listener's mind's eye are not implicit in its pure sound environment. These responses are daydreams, programmatically triggered by an individual's own range of personal experience, by undirected or lazy listening habits, and perhaps by associations deep-rooted in childhood. (1975: 74)

Bazelon suggests here that music speaks only in and of its own aesthetics; according to him, music is both nonrepresentational and nonreferential. Bazelon, Adorno, Stravinsky, and many other writers on music thus contend that meanings heard in music stem simply from the bad habits of listeners who have not been trained properly.

Recent music scholarship suggests otherwise. But even if we were to accept Bazelon, Adorno, and Stravinsky at face value about most musics, film music would still raise questions. Film music has always depended on communicating meaning; in terms of the western art music tradition from which it stems, it is a special case.

From the very beginnings of film to the present, music for film accompaniment has been catalogued according to subject and emotion. An organist in a silent movie house might well have turned to Erno Rapee's *Encyclopaedia of Music for Pictures* (1925), and would have found such categories as "Aeroplane," "Oriental," and "Sinister." A contemporary corporation producing in-house industrial videos (used for sales, marketing, and training) can turn to a production music library such as Network Music. Production music libraries are recorded collections of music indexed by mood (e.g., romantic, eerie, light), geography (Western, oriental, panoramic), time (historical, contemporary, futuristic), genre (classical, rock, marches), structural function (introductions, links), and action (travel, crime, sport). In such a library, directors, multimedia presentation authors, and others can find very much the same possibilities that Rapee's collection offered, with the advantage that they are prerecorded and indexed in a database. Our corporation (or film/video student or market analyst or low-budget film/video producer) can now "rent" music, complete with meaning, for "Fanfare," "Space," or "Fashion."[1]

Most film music scholars assume that classical Hollywood film music is a communicative system that can be "read" by listeners. For some, the position that film music is a meaning system requires no support. For instance, in *Unheard Melodies: Narrative Film Music*, Claudia Gorbman performs a commutation on a bicycling sequence from *Jules et Jim*, which means she describes what would happen to that sequence if a series of single aspects of the score were altered. A minor mode would make the scene sadder, an increase in tempo would make the bicycling seem faster and the sequence more optimistic, an orchestration change might lend more pathos (solo violin) or humor (solo tuba), and so forth (1987: 16–17). This commutation makes sense—and there's no doubt that it does—because we all understand classical

Hollywood scoring and can easily imagine the effect these score changes would have.

Descriptions of film music such as this one serve at least as a convenient shorthand. They have by far the most connection with how listeners actually perceive film music: they function somehow subliminally or subconsciously, evoking meanings and moods rather than explaining ideas.

On the other hand, most descriptions tend to be too broad, encompassing a constellation of meanings rather than a narrower one. For example, Frith (1984) lists some "casual musical descriptions: 'middle-of-the-road,' 'background,' 'up-beat,' 'Close Encounters climactic,' 'new-exciting-world-just-around-the-corner,' 'youth music,' 'homely, healthy, folky'" (1984: 83). His "Close Encounters climactic" most likely includes (at least) epic-scale, high-tech or futuristic, and climactic. Each of those meanings corresponds to musical features that can be agglomerated to form "Close Encounters climactic," but might also be combined with other elements to produce other constellations of meanings: epic seafaring, futuristic sexuality, etc.

More detailed analyses do exist. Kalinak (1982) has shown some of the elements that communicate the only two female sexualities—the fallen woman and the virtuous wife—that Hollywood imagined in the forties and fifties. She describes the genres, instrumentations, rhythms, melodic shapes, and harmonic languages specific to each stereotyped woman. While the fallen woman gets dotted rhythms, increased chromaticism, and saxes, often in jazz or blues style, the virtuous wife's violins and flutes sweep upward melodically in even rhythms and lush but simple harmonic language.

Kalinak's brief study is supported by empirical research done by Tagg and Clarida (n.d.); their study describes in detail how film music communicates certain meanings.[2] Tagg asked listeners to respond to ten film and television title themes by writing down what they saw or imagined while listening.[3] Tagg and Clarida then grouped the responses and began to correlate them to musical features. Taken individually, responses varied quite widely. Grouped together, however, they read like descriptions of the series or film to which the theme belonged, particularly in regard to genre and style.

For example, the theme to the TV series *Miami Vice* was played to 105 respondents, who produced a total of 328 verbal-visual associations. While no one reported recognizing the tune, the music indicated aggression, speed, and urban environments to most listeners. No one heard qualities like reflection, love, ritual, religion, or animals. Thirty percent of the listeners heard clubs (discos, bars, nightclubs), 28 percent heard cars, 24 percent heard chases, and 20 percent heard dynamism, using words such as "excitement" and "action." Fifteen percent heard young people, and 12 percent heard youth subcultural ideas such as "rebellious," "cool," and "rad." Similarly, responses to Alex North's theme for *A Streetcar Named Desire* included "drama," "bar," "threat," "slum," "1940s," "1950s," "struggle," "smoky," "intense," "tension," "night," "sweat," "underworld," and "excitement." In other words, the verbal-visual associations for a theme sum up the show's terrain quite neatly.

A comparison of the respondents' associations with those in a mood music catalogue points out the stability of film music's meaning system. Using the question of gender as an example, I calculated the frequency with which respondents "saw" either men or women in the scenes they imagined in relation to the themes, correlated those responses to other categories, and compared those correlations to mood music catalogue titles. For instance, in the themes the listeners identified as female-associated, 27 percent wrote "rural" associations, making this a highly feminine category. In the Selected Sounds mood music catalogue, tunes with women's names appear most frequently in the category "Pastoral/Romantic." Mood music cataloguers and the respondents to the Tagg and Clarida study make similar—and similarly gendered—associations with music.

Tagg and Clarida's study, especially in connection with mood music catalogues, suggests that in mass-market, narrative film music, correspondence between producer's intention and consumer's reading, between transmission and reception, between encoding and decoding, and among decodings, is high—so high that it seems safe to conclude that it can support using strategies from communications and linguistics. On the other hand, it is important to remember that the responses to this study were by no means identical. In other words, as in language or any other code, there is a certain degree of consistency among productions and receptions, but not complete consistency, and the relationship between productions and receptions is by no means either simple or unidirectional.

The skill that generates consistency in encodings and decodings of film music is "competence." Clearly, competence in this sense can only function for speakers (and listeners) of the same language (or musical genre[4]), and the consistency will vary according to fluency (extent of experience in the genre), personal history, etc. Competence is a culturally acquired skill possessed to varying degrees in varying genres by all hearing people in a given culture.

The notion of competence must be distinguished from literacy. Together, these terms raise some important questions about the absence of music in film theory and the possibilities for finding ways to include it. As was the case in Tagg and Clarida's study, and as Adorno has argued, the "subjective content of a musical experience" is difficult to discern:

Experiments may tell us about degrees of the intensity of the reaction; they will hardly reach its quality.... Besides, most people who have not mastered the technical terminology will encounter insurmountable obstacles in verbalizing their own musical experiences, quite apart from the fact that the verbal expression itself is already prefiltered and its value for a knowledge of primary reactions is thus doubly questionable. (1988: 4)

The language for discussing music to which Adorno is referring is that of institutionalized music studies: European art music composition, performance, theory, and musicology. Competence in this particular language for music is what I'm calling here literacy. It has a very specific ideological history of its own, and has created a situation in which music can be spoken of only in terms of its intramusical features: form, harmonic language, orchestration, etc. The discourse of musical analysis has, in other words, interiorized itself, so that only trained musicians and music scholars are literate, are permitted to speak about music—and never in terms of the extramusical associations that nonprofessionals generally understand as the music's meaning.

This discursive sleight-of-hand has had many consequences for musicians and musics. Peter Winkler has suggested that it leads immediately to assignments of value:

Many Western musicians think of a piece of music not in terms of musical sounds but in terms of a musical *score*.... This essentially "visualist" orientation can be seen as an outgrowth of the high value Western culture places on visual evidence in general and writing in particular. Such an orientation easily leads to ethnocentrism. In the curricula of many of our music schools, "musicianship" is synonymous with "musical literacy": the clear implication is that if you can't read music, you are not really a

musician. And music that does not rely on a notated score for its
transmission tends to be seen as an abnormality, a musical "other,"
something that is not really, or not fully, music. (1997: 171)

(In the world of contemporary film music, Danny Elfman became
a magnet for such dismissals. David Mermelstein wrote in the *New
York Times*, "Ask about composers who have prospered despite a
lack of formal training, and the first name to come up is Danny
Elfman's." Elfman is not fully, smoothly, comfortably literate in
music, a fact that has caused a whirlwind of controversy about his
work. And yet, Elfman's scores make a great deal of money in
both box office and soundtrack album sales, and they display not
only sophistication but also a sense of humor.)

As Stockfelt has argued, there have been consequences not only
for music making but also for listening as well. Listening practices
that were developed in the latter part of the nineteenth century
have become institutionalized as "culturally superior," and have
conditioned analytical practices that are not now (and may never
have been) applicable to everyday listening:

In a way, a relatively functional explicit language has been created,
in verbal and graphic form, to describe the experiencing and experiences of a certain type of music, of a certain type of listening. This
language, to some extent and for lack of better alternatives, could
be used to communicate verbally and graphically even around
other forms of listening. This language has hence become one of
the material prerequisites for the development of communication and value-systems around music even in environments that
show few external similarities with the bourgeois idealized concert hall. (1997: 162)

Stockfelt has proposed that, in order to analyze everyday music experiences, one must "develop one's reflexive consciousness and competence as an active 'idle listener.'" Film music competence, as opposed to literacy, requires just such a rethinking of analytical tools.

Competence is based on decipherable codes learned through experience. As with language and visual image, we learn through exposure what a given tempo, series of notes, key, time signature, rhythm, volume, and orchestration are meant to signify.[5] But the acquisition and modus operandi of competence are rarely questioned or examined. Film composers have spoken in interviews and books about scoring films, discussing the various musical techniques and elements that carry specific messages. For example, Bazelon, himself a composer who has done some work in film, uses a series of unquestioned categories to describe the effects of music in particular moments:

> To this day the opening to *Citizen Kane* (1941) remains a brilliant example of the total fusion of music, sound, and symbolistic imagery. Bernard Herrmann's low, ominous array of sounds intones dramatic doom . . . the music evokes portentous associations and feelings of awe at the vacuous grandeur of God-Kane's castle. Extraneous voices and echoing sounds act as counterpoint, enriching the tonal ambience and enhancing the images. (1975: 98)

While Bazelon can describe the elements that make the music "intone dramatic doom," it does not seem to occur to him to question how or why we know that this is so. Gorbman's commutation of the *Jules et Jim* sequence described above functions similarly; she assumes the changes she suggests would be interpreted similarly by others.

As I suggested earlier, these writers are all quite reasonably assuming the results of studies such as Kalinak's and Tagg and

Clarida's. Within the realm of classical film scoring, with its reliance on late-Romantic (especially German) art music practices, most members of western cultures are competent. Audiences have simply seen enough films to know what "low, ominous sounds" or tubas mean. While this still does not answer the question of how tubas have become humorous, it does give us a beginning for a different kind of analysis of film music. Once we acknowledge that we understand these codes similarly, we can begin to work out ways of talking about music that may not be sanctioned by institutionalized academic music practices, but will permit film scholars to institutionalize music as part of analyses of films. We can develop, in other words, a language of musical competence.

But the same information and arguments that support this notion of competence also point to the existence of a communicative system; the two are mutually dependent.

Music and Discourse Analysis

Communication can only take place through a set of cultural conventions through which one member of a society communicates—that is, interacts socially through messages—with herself or another member of that same society (Fiske 1982: 1–3). The study of communication requires a vocabulary for elements of its functioning, including language specific to analysis of its code; such language has been developed in semiotics for language and film, but less so in music.

In his first major work, Tagg included an extensive list of musical parameters for use in locating and analyzing these features of music (1979). It enumerates forty-three different features of any single example of music, from time and timbre to acoustics and studio effects. While now long out of date, this list is one important way that Tagg's work differs from that of the few other semioticians of music (e.g., Nattiez 1975). It ensures a careful examination of each aspect of a musical event, including the signifying features of technological manipulation. This is particularly important for semiotic studies of film music, since technological manipulation makes possible, for example, the production of space that Gorbman describes in her still singular study of *Sous les toits de Paris* (1987: 140–50). In this sense, such a list encourages examination of the meaning produced by all aspects of a musical instance, rather than just traditional musicological or music theoretical features.

For example, in an eleven-page discussion of the theme from the TV series *Miami Vice*, Clarida (in Tagg and Clarida) analyzes the musical sources of the effects and associations of the study's respondents described above. He accounts for the extremely high appearance of associations such as "chase," "action," and "rebellious" as follows:

> To return to the "inhospitable"/"aggressive" scenario, which was far more common among our *Miami Vice* listeners, we may wish to begin by considering the referential function of the percussion sounds which have concerned us so far. The bongos and the "hi-hat" noise of the introduction aren't likely to contribute much to this negative scenario for several reasons....
>
> The timbales, for all their fashionability, may contribute quite a lot to the grim interpretation, though. In particular, the initial timbale entrance at m.2 (a loud, low, reverberant boom which completely obscures m.1's high, dry ticking) is in keeping with a long tradition of sharp attack, low register doom sounds: Frank Skinner's 1950 *Underscore* refers on page 13 to a low register sforzando-piano as a "menace" note, and Erno Rapee's 1924 *Motion Picture Moods for Pianists and Organists* catalogs Beethoven's *Coriolan Overture*, with its opening of long fortissimo low C's, under "Sinister." (n.d.: "Miami Vice," 6–7)

This is precisely the kind of musical discourse analysis that reception studies should generate. Clarida begins by considering what the musical reasons might be for the associations the listeners made, and having located a possible source of these associations, examines the source carefully both intrinsically and extrinsically. In this way, he is able to place particular musical features in a larger field of musical discourse that is embedded in social interaction; he describes this instance of music, in other words, as an act of communication.

But musical discourse analysis has some limitations as well. While music and language are both semiotic codes,[6] unlike students of language, music scholars have no equivalent of a dictionary of musemes (the smallest unit of musical meaning) or museme compounds as a starting point, nor are there any parallels to language-to-language dictionaries available. (For example, while one can find dictionaries to translate between distant members of the same language family, such as English-Armenian within Indo-European languages, what would a ska–late Romanticism dictionary be, even though both are members of the tonal musical language family?) Nor is there a thesaurus available to suggest "synonyms," nor a source for "etymological" information on the roots of musemes. Moreover, any attempt to create these resources would necessarily be limited by the differences between music and language. Museme compounds, even within specific musical genres, have even less stable values than words. There are more variables to alter musemes than there are letters and intonation variables with which to alter words.

(Another way to express the difference between verbal language and music is in terms of computer space: a basic MIDI file of a six-track rock tune lasting two minutes and twenty-five seconds, stripped of formatting, takes up 18kb.[7] A page of verbal text without formatting, which would take about the same length of time to read, is a 2–3kb file. Even in traditional notation, one minute of sound takes eight pages of a thirty-two-part score versus twelve or so lines of verbal text. Music packs "information" much more densely than words.)

There are also at least two consequences of this aspect of the history of music studies that bear mentioning here. First, there is no immediately apparent way to dislodge the widespread notion that each piece of music is ultimately new, more new and created from much "rawer" material than, for example, a work of literature.[8] Second, the relatively fleeting appearance and disappearance of work on the semiotics of music and the nature of its limitations mean that any "etymological" efforts would be necessarily speculative.

Music and Ideology Critique

Since the difficulties of analyzing music and meaning persist, the recognition that musical communication bears ideologies is still struggling for acceptance. Adorno, Stravinsky, and Bazelon all seem to suggest that music is outside of social relations, pure in some fundamental, ontological way. These ideas appear in film music scholarship as well, as when Gorbman refers to

> that abstract arrangement and rearrangement of sound which is music, [which] is nonrepresentational and non-narrative.... If we listen to a Bach fugue, independently of any other activity, we are listening to the functioning of *pure musical codes*, generating musical discourse; music on this level refers to musical structure itself. (1987: 12–13)

A comparable statement about a piece of literature, or even a non-narrative film, would be difficult to imagine. Gorbman sets aside here the historical context: during the Baroque period the sense of time was shifting from a circular to a linear view. Notions of "progress" were relatively new—as were the directional harmonic progressions known as tonal harmony, which precede the directional structure of sonata form by fifty or more years. In short, even a Bach fugue has ideological markings, and does not simply refer "to musical structure itself."

Examples of how ideologies function in "absolute" music are numerous. But are music practices and dominant ideologies mutually constitutive? Theo van Leeuwen argues that while music is generally considered to elicit only emotional responses, it can and does do ideological work as well. He suggests that "music makes us apprehend what are, in themselves, 'nonemotional' meanings *in an emotional way,* that it binds us affectively to these meanings and makes us identify with them" (1988: 21). He argues that various musical systems such as meter, key center, and interval size encode meanings about social organization. While it is not explicitly van Leeuwen's project to suggest that music and social organizations create each other, this point is implicit in each of his discussions.

His argument concerning the rise to dominance of major tonality, for instance, makes a strong case for the mutuality of musical expressions of ideologies and their developments in society:

> Major tonality came to the fore as the unmarked option, the "normal," and in a sense normative tonality in Western art music in the late Middle Ages. Before that time the ideologically dominant music, the music of the Church, shunned the Ionian mode (which corresponds to our present major) although that mode was widely used in secular music.... The ascendance of major, then, was linked to a gradual but irreversible shift in cultural hegemony from the Church to the rising merchant class, and major

came to be associated with what could be called the positive values of that class: belief in progress through human achievement, science, industry, exploration, and so on. (1988: 21–22)

At the same time as the merchant class was gaining power, composers of church music began to include works written in major keys; the new music and the new class rose to dominance together. (In fact, for a long period in the history of the Roman Catholic Church, the Vatican issued statements as to the permissibility of compositional practices. The popes seem to have known what western society since the Enlightenment has tried to repress—that musics and social orders are connected.)

In very much the same way, film music constitutes society while being constituted by it. The well-established code communicates groupings of ideas that are associated with each other in dominant ideologies, and by communicating these groupings on a nonconscious level, the code can buttress and reproduce the very ideologies that produced it. In the case of film music, van Leeuwen's hearing in an emotional way is crucial to how that music communicates ideologies, because it makes the ideological work seem personal or private and thus removes the messages from the realms of the political, social, or public.

There are, in fact, a number of ways that ideology critique can be connected to any instance of music. First, there are critiques of the ideology *of* music that analyze features of how we think about music, the conditions under which we receive music, the assumptions we make about it, and so on. Van Leeuwen's hearing in an emotional way is an example of this category of work, as is Kalinak's chapter on sound and vision (1992). Second, critiques of ideology *in* music, such as my passing remarks above on Baroque forms, unpack how specifically musical procedures bear ideological meanings. Third, critiques of ideologies communicated *by*

music include all the features Fabbri (1982) describes as genre and
Stockfelt (1993) discusses in terms of adequate listening practices.
These include not only textual musical features, but also all the
extramusical features that come to be associated with particular
musical styles or gestures. This is, of course, a matter of approach
and priority, not of absolute distinction; each aspect of the relationship between ideology and music operates at the same time
in and during every musical event. However, earlier I left a thread with
its priority on ideology critique of the third type dangling; it is time
now to pick it up again.

In examining the Tagg and Clarida study, I found that their listeners predominantly associated certain ideas, such as tranquility,
with women, or strength with men. Others, such as quiescence,
were exclusively associated with women, just as weapons, for
instance, were with men.[9] In other words, in no theme did listeners imagine both female characters and weapons, or male characters and a quiescent scene or mood. In terms of feminist theory, it
is immediately clear that these associations, in addition to align-
ing comfortably with mood music catalogue categories, fit very
neatly with various founding theories of gender difference and
power relations. What follows may seem surprisingly simplistic
and outdated in relation to contemporary feminist theoretical
work. But while gendered identities and their articulations in culture may be quite complex, respondents in this study heard a very
untroubled and traditional regime of gender. (For an analysis of
production music and corporate masculinity, see Fink 2000.)

The three most obvious theoretical alignments of the responses
are with early feminist theories of the opposition of nature/culture,
the association of female characters with plot-space, and the ideology of separate spheres. Theorists of the nature/culture dichotomy
argued that women in the cultural imagination are connected with

nature: reproduction, maternal instinct, the body, "earthiness," witchcraft, etc. Men are associated with culture: production, art, architecture, law, social order, technology, modern medicine, etc.

Table 1 in appendix A shows how these associations appeared in the study;[10] the differences in the categories "rural" and "urban" are particularly striking. The study's respondents were absolutely sure that female characters belong in "green" settings while male characters are most at home in concrete. They strongly associated women with nature and men with culture. The themes in which listeners heard female characters and rural settings also registered high in the category "romantic." Musical analysis of these themes revealed that:

> The pastoral and rural are ideologically more steeped in history than the urban and industrial. This means that pastoral music will tend—as we see from responses—to connote yesteryear rather than modern life or future space travel. Pastoral music must therefore—from the receiver's hearpoint—contain some archaism. In our test pieces archaism was: (1) instrumental/timbric—none of the "female" examples contain any rock drum sets, rhythm machines, electric guitars, etc.; (2) harmonic—none of the decisively "male" examples contain directional classical harmony; (3) gestural ("phrasing")—all motivic figures in the "female" examples are phrased *legato* and rounded off; (4) rhythmic—no "female" examples contain inverted dottings or downbeat anticipations [i.e., what is generally termed "syncopation"]. (Tagg and Clarida, n.d.)

Pastorality, then, has to do with the feminine and with the preindustrial, not with Golden Gate or Hyde Parks. Respondents also heard pastorality as resolutely European (western); each of the

musical features described above is quite closely associated with
western art ("classical") music and therefore with high culture.

In mood music catalogues, nature relates intimately to pastorality, romance, leisure, and scenic grandeur (Tagg n.d., 11). It
also overlaps with categories like "ethnic," "heroic," "melancholy/
sad," "religious," and "children." Science and technology oppose
nature, and while nature is calm and peaceful, science and technology are frightening (pp. 13–24). The many aspects of dominant
ideologies expressed in these associations and oppositions include:
(1) that the ethnic (i.e., nonwhite, non-western) is natural and
pleasurable, (2) that history is idyllic and progress is threatening,
and (3) that romance does not belong in or to environments of
human construction. (Each of these is expressed in thousands
of other cultural productions, from clothing ads to science-fiction
movies to historical preservation society brochures.)

It is here that Kalinak's virtuous wife and Tagg's pastoral nature
meet. The features to which Tagg attributes the musical meaning
"pastoral" are also the features that Kalinak says represent the
virtuous wife: no syncopation, directional classical harmonies, and
legato phrasing. Since these features belong in particular to the
music of high culture, and since the ideologies they represent
define particular class relations (pastorality suggests a leisure-class
relation to nature, and Hollywood's virtuous wife was always a
homemaker), they mark the mutual imbrication of class and
gender. Not only does the associative conglomerate woman-
nature-romance that the respondents heard serve to support the
strength of feminist theories, it also points out how intertwined
ideologies are and how intricate film music's code can be.

But the gendered relations of space are not confined to the
nature versus culture dichotomy. Lotman argues that there are
only two character types, and these are defined by their relationship to plot-space:

Characters can be divided into those who are mobile, who enjoy freedom with regard to plot-space, who can change their place in the structure of the artistic world and cross the frontier, the basic topological feature of this space, and those who are immobile, who represent, in fact, a function of this space. . . . [Narrative is a simple chain of two functions:] entry into a closed space, and emergence from it. . . . Closed space can be interpreted as "a cave," "the grave," "a house," "woman" (and, correspondingly, be allotted the features of darkness, warmth, dampness). . . . (1979: 167)

Several points bear examination here, according to de Lauretis. The first is that mobile characters (heroes) must be men, since immobile characters, features of the topological space, are morphologically women. Consequently, men act, cross boundaries, and so forth, while women accept the hero's entry into and emergence from the space they represent (1984: 118–19). Reflections of this structure in the study's responses appear in table 2 (see appendix A). In light of the responses in the categories "reflection" and "dynamism" alone, it is clear that, for the study's respondents, men move and act, while women sit by quietly and patiently. One interesting feature of this table is the "zero categories." No listener heard any ideas of "destiny" or "against the will of" in themes in which they heard male characters, nor did they hear ideas of "culturally emergent" in songs in which they heard female characters. They were clear, in other words, that male characters have control over their own "lives," including control over the possibility of resistance or rebellion, while the "immobility" Lotman ascribed to plot-space is quite clearly expressed as characteristic of female characters.

The second point that de Lauretis makes regarding Lotman's typology is that human beings are defined as men, and everything else is "not even 'woman,' but not-man, an absolute abstraction"

(1984: 121). This was also clear to the study's respondents: by a huge margin, they found it easiest to imagine a single individual as specifically male, and in general found it difficult indeed to picture specifically female people in the scenes they imagined. This is, of course, related to the "men act and women sit" distinction; humans (male characters) are agents of narratives, individual/individuated subjects, and consequently easier to imagine, whereas female characters, who are static, nonhuman features of plot-space, do not necessarily come to mind in describing a scene. Of course, the more frequent visualization of "several males" than of "couples" or females (in any number) suggests that Hollywood film music belongs to a highly homosocial realm in which narrative is predicated on action, action is predicated on masculinity, and female characters are both unnecessary and undesirable. The containment of female characters in this scene serves not only patriarchal ideologies, but also heterosexist ones.

For the study's listeners, this ideological containment included not only narratological concerns and the nature/culture split, but also the division of labor in the idealized middle-class nuclear family. The distinction between the private sphere and the public sphere, a distinction most fully developed by Marxist theorists, is connected to gender ideology by the construction of a gendered division of labor and space.[11] With the rise of the capitalist mode of production came the ideology of the separation of state and economy. Supporting this separation was the ideology of separate spheres: the public and the private. The public sphere includes forms for the free exchange of ideas (e.g., newspapers, town meetings) and social space (e.g., the park, the town square), and is male. The private sphere, also known as the domestic sphere, includes the home and all of its associations (e.g., food, clothing, child-rearing, affective values), and is female.

There are, of course, strong connections between the public/

private distinction and Lotman's plot typology; women are confined to a specific space, and actually come to represent that space itself. Table 4 shows how separate spheres ideologies appeared in the study. The overwhelming association between women and love assures that affective values are still ideologically the domain of women, and that emotions are still not permitted to spill over into any other sphere. (This is one way that the doctrine of objectivity reproduces itself.) Moreover, the strong connection between the "maleness" of tunes and the public activities of the categories "festive" and "presentational" demonstrates that the public/private distinction still operates and still encodes gendered ideologies.

As may by now be apparent, there are certain important places where all of these descriptions of ideologies of gender meet. Woman, the figure of the female, is strongly associated with romance; not only is she necessary for a romantic scene to exist (in part a marker of both the heterosexist and masculinist biases of films and our culture in general), but her very image—visual or musical—connotes romance itself. As Gorbman writes:

> A film of the forties is airing on television. Even though you're in the next room, you are likely to find that a certain kind of music will cue you in correctly to the presence of Woman on screen. It is as if the emotional excess of this presence must find its outlet in the euphony of a string orchestra. I refer here to Woman as romantic Good Object, and not to old women, or humorous or chatty women, or femmes fatales (who possess their own musical conventions—jazz, brass, woodwinds . . .). (1987: 80)

Gorbman makes an important distinction here between the abstract idea/ideal of the Hollywood heroine and other female characters. These other women are, however, predominantly limited to supporting "character" roles (meaning, in large part, roles devoid of sexuality). On the issue of woman and romance, the study's participants, the mood music catalogues, and gender theories all converge. Woman is the object (plot-space) of man's desire (she provokes the primal—the "natural"—in him), the bearer of affective (private sphere) values.

There is, of course, much more to say about ideologies of gender and their articulations in music (see, for some now classic examples, McClary 1991, and Solie 1993.) My point here, however, is that classical Hollywood film music is a semiotic code, and that it can and should be subjected to various semiotic and cultural studies methods, such as discourse analysis and ideology critique. Such studies would not only further scholarly understandings of classical Hollywood film, but would also intervene in important ways in debates about music and meaning in musicology, communications, sociology, music theory, ethnomusicology, philosophy, and popular music studies.

But analyzing film music outside of the context of the film from which it is taken is only a first step, because the meanings the music bears are produced in conjunction with all other aspects of the film. It is to the relationships among these threads that I turn in chapter 2.

2

How Music Works in Film

ilm criticism has historically been concerned with the visual
and narrative aspects of fiction film, for the most part omit-
ting any serious discussion of the score and its relationship
to the film as a whole. I have argued elsewhere (Kassabian 1994)
that—in part because of film studies' visual bias—the groundwork has been laid for the serious study of film music in the
English language only in recent years.[1] The important textual,
historical, and theoretical studies of Gorbman, Kalinak, Flinn,
Brown, Marks, and Smith make it possible and fruitful now to
consider other kinds of questions about film music, such as what
film perceivers hear. In particular, this chapter turns to the range
of relations perceivers may hear in a single event of film music—
relations among image track, narrative, sound effects, dialogue,
and music.

In "What is Cultural Studies Anyway?" Johnson (1987) argues
that most theories and methodologies describe a view from a particular moment of cultural processes. The circuit of a cultural
object's existence, he says, consists of four "moments": production,
texts, readings, and lived cultures/social relations.[2] In this chapter, I will suggest that the schemes produced thus far by theorists
of film music have belonged to other moments on the circuit,
and never to reading, which I call here perception.

Since the early history of film, film scholars have attempted to describe the possible relationships between music and visuals. Historically, film theorists generally relegated the music to one of two possibilities: parallelism or counterpoint.[3] Of the small handful of books that attempt serious analyses of film music, most have also included some outline of how music and visuals work together. Broadly speaking, these descriptions have fallen into two categories, of which two books will serve as paradigmatic examples: *Composing for the Films* by Hanns Eisler and Theodor Adorno (1947),[4] and *Unheard Melodies: Narrative Film Music* by Claudia Gorbman (1987). Eisler and Adorno represent the group of critics and theorists who treat film music at the moment of production, as an "art," whereas Gorbman's book exemplifies a kind of criticism at the moment of text that is prevalent in film studies.

The first two paragraphs of *Composing for the Films* display the Eisler/Adorno position succinctly. These two hundred words contain all the features of Adorno's theories of culture that have been elaborately critiqued over the past two decades:

- The dismissal of popular culture as the product of an oppressive "culture industry" (scoring clichés "only seem to make sense as a consequence of standardization within the industry itself, which calls for standard practices everywhere" [p. 3]);
- The assumption that art has its own narrative, progressive logic of development (scoring clichés "originated in the intellectual milieu of Tin Pan Alley; and because of practical considerations and problems of personnel, they have so entrenched themselves that they, more than anything else, have hindered the progress of motion-picture music" [p. 3]);
- The contention that ideology is false consciousness that could be overcome by educating the masses ("Public realization of the antiquated character of these rules should suffice to break their hold" [p. 3]).

These are not, however, the only issues of concern here. Eisler and Adorno's position on music as a semiotic system bears directly on how they imagine film music should sound. By calling on "developments in ... autonomous music," they inherit a history—discussed in the previous chapter—of music as nonrepresentational. While the second appendix to *Composing for the Films* is a composition by Eisler entitled "Fourteen ways to describe rain," on page 20 they state that

> music is supposed to bring out the spontaneous, essentially human element in its listeners and in virtually all human relations. As the abstract art *par excellence,* and as the art farthest removed from the world of practical things, it is predestined to perform this function.

Even though in *Introduction to the Sociology of Music* Adorno calls music "a language without concepts" (p. 44), he and Eisler dismiss standardization within the film music industry as if languages of any sort were not sets of conventions. By understanding music as an art rather than as a meaning-making practice, Eisler and Adorno contain it within the realm of the universal and the aesthetic, and remove perceivers even as part of the evaluative process of film music.

All of this takes place within the first two pages of the book, which is also the beginning of the first chapter, "Prejudices and Bad Habits." They go on to enumerate the bad habits of the title—most of which reappear in every description of music in film since the 1930s: The Leitmotif (pp. 4–6), Melody and Euphony (pp. 6–9), Unobtrusiveness (pp. 9–11), Visual Justification (pp. 11–12), Illustration (pp. 12–14), Geography and History (pp. 14–15), Stock Music (pp. 15–16), Clichés (pp. 16–18), and Standardized Interpretations (pp. 18–19). But because perceivers do not drive Eisler and

Adorno's prescriptions for film scores, the two theorists can dismiss these practices as bad habits in spite of the extent to which perceivers rely on them for understanding not only film music, but also films as wholes.

Narratology and film theory, rather than Frankfurt School theories of culture, motor Gorbman's model. She identifies seven principles of the composition, mixing, and editing of music in classical film, summarizing them as follows:

I. *Invisibility:* The technical apparatus of nondiegetic music must not be visible.

II. *"Inaudibility":* Music is not meant to be heard consciously. As such it should subordinate itself to dialogue, to visuals—i.e., to the primary vehicles of the narrative.

III. *Signifier of emotion:* Soundtrack music may set specific moods and emphasize particular emotions suggested in the narrative, but first and foremost, it is a signifier of emotion itself.

IV. *Narrative cueing:*
    referential/narrative: Music gives referential and narrative cues, e.g., indicating point of view, supplying formal demarcations, and establishing setting and characters.
    connotative: Music "interprets" and "illustrates" narrative events.

V. *Continuity:* Music provides formal and rhythmic continuity— between shots, in transitions between scenes, by filling "gaps."

VI. *Unity:* Via repetition and variation of musical material and instrumentation, music aids in the construction of formal and narrative unity.

VII. A given film score may violate any of the principles above, providing that violation is at the service of the other principles. (p. 73)

This model clearly delineates some of the most important features of classical film music's "laws." The problem is that each principle isolates one aspect of the process of film music's functions, but only one. As a signifier of emotion, for example, music undoubtedly makes strong suggestions of how perceivers should feel about a particular scene, but Gorbman's scheme does not allow for differences in perceivers' relations to the music, nor for how they might differ in perception of meaning and emotion when the specific scene is analyzed as an entire unit. Nor, in her discussion of the referential/narrative cueing that is one of film music's major functions, does she suggest how differently perceivers might interpret cues that establish setting.

Gorbman does not consider these issues because her analysis resides firmly within the text moment of film music's circulation. She considers the music in relation to the narrative world of the film; that narrative world has been unhinged theoretically from authorial intention but not connected thereby to audience reception. At stake for Gorbman is a theoretical object frozen before the moment of reading. The scores she analyzes are absented from historical and subjective listening conditions and belong to the films analyzed by a long tradition of film scholars with similar concerns and approaches.

I do not dismiss interventions at these and other moments. But because I intervene in the circulation of films as musical texts at the moment of perception, this chapter neither evaluates and prescribes compositional practices, nor analyzes them as elements of narrative. Instead, I locate three fundamental questions that, from the perception perspective, need to be asked about the music in a film sequence:

- How is the music's relationship to the narrative world of the film perceived?

- How do we perceive the music's method within the scene?
- What does the music evoke in or communicate to us?

I will discuss each of these questions separately before considering their interrelationships.

Music and the Narrative: Is There Only In or Out?

Film critics typically discuss the question of music's relationship to the narrative world of the film in terms of diegetic versus nondiegetic music. Diegetic music is music that is produced within the implied world of the film; we can specify or assume where and by what characters the music is produced. Nondiegetic music is produced from some unspecified external source. While this distinction is not only standard but also useful in explaining narrative functions of music, it institutes some troubling ideas about film music.

First, it describes a "film," prior to the music, that constructs its narratively implied world silently. This clearly cannot be the case, since music (and sound more generally) contribute significantly to the construction of spatial relations and time passage in narrative films. Gorbman's analysis of *Sous les toits de Paris* demonstrates quite clearly a musical construction of diegetic space, while Kalinak's analysis of *Captain Blood* exemplifies the importance of music as a signifier of passing time and as an anchor of continuous time. The distinction between diegetic and nondiegetic music thus obscures music's role in producing the diegesis itself.

Second, it suggests that film music can be categorized within a dichotomous schema—grossly reduced as either "in" (diegetic) or "out" (nondiegetic) of the narrative world of the film. This dichotomy is insufficient; it cannot comfortably describe music that seems to fall "in between" these categories, much less account for its different character. Perhaps more importantly, it shifts critical attention away from features of the music—through its ability to match cues with the visual track—that coincide with the different possible narrative statuses.

Many film theorists who have considered the relationship between the score and the narrative come from a background in literary theory, and have tended to treat this issue in dichotomous terms because they consider it in terms of narratology. Even Shumway, who points out the problem, retains the categories in service of the primacy and preexistence of the narrative. In his discussion of *American Graffiti*, he points out:

> Given the ubiquity of the music and the fact that its volume changes without clear narrative explanation (e.g., the music is always loud when we get an establishing shot of Mel's Burger World, but the volume then decreases to allow conversation to be foregrounded), we cannot classify the music in *American Graffiti* as straightforwardly diegetic even though the movie wants the viewer to assume its quasi-diegetic origin. Rather, the line between diegetic and nondiegetic is impossible to establish. (1999: 41)

And yet he retains the language diegetic/nondiegetic, reinforcing the notion that there is a diegesis before the music. A textual analysis such as his concerns itself with issues more suited to such a distinction than an analysis from the moment of reading.

Film composers, who are not overtly theorists and who stand at the moment of production, divide film music along different lines. In *Scoring for Films*, a handbook for film composers, Earle Hagen describes three different types of scoring. He outlines the categories standardly used by the industry: *source music, source scoring,* and *pure* or *dramatic scoring* (1971: 90). The term *source music* corresponds roughly to the term *diegetic music;* both terms refer to music whose production is within the narrative world of the film. For example, the music in the bar sequence in *Star Wars* is source or diegetic music. While Luke and Ben are trying to contact a pilot, the source of the songs—a group of nonhuman musicians—is shown producing the music within the narrative itself.

According to Hagen's definitions, this is visual source music, precisely because we see them playing. There is a fairly long series of shots in the bar before they are revealed, however, during which time the music is implied source music. Because we can infer the source of this kind of music in that kind of bar, we know the music exists within the narrative world of the film, even though we don't *see* its source. It is implied that there are musicians playing on some unseen stage. (It is interesting to note here that the music in this scene is a kind of upbeat major key Dixieland-style quartet. Unlike the music for the Ewok celebration at the end of *The Return of the Jedi*, this jazz does not attempt to be alien, even though none of the musicians and few of the patrons are humans.)

Source music rarely matches cues with the rest of the film. It does not, for example, stop for a particularly dramatic moment in the dialogue. The narrative event must be extraordinary in order for source music to attend to it, and even then the music responds to the event rather than matching it. In the above-mentioned sequence in *Star Wars*, for example, the music stops when the murderer and Ben begin to fight, and resumes after Ben cuts off the murderer's arm. The music responds to the event because the musicians' attention is demanded by the event: they stop playing.

Dramatic scoring is Hagen's term for nondiegetic music: it is not produced within the narrative world of the film. According to Hagen, "Pure scoring, or Dramatic scoring, is the granddaddy of the three principal techniques. . . . The first note you play represents total dramatic license." Much of what we think of as film music falls into this category—the strings behind the kiss, the fast-paced action music behind car chases, the opening sequence of *Star Wars* when the Imperial troops invade Princess Leia's ship.

Dramatic scoring maximally matches the visual events on the screen. The "shark" theme from *Jaws*, for example, intensifies as the shark gets closer to the swimmer, and climaxes at the moment of attack. Rather than being organized as a reaction to other events in the film, dramatic scoring moves concurrently with the action. Dramatic scoring includes many film music clichés. The *Jaws* theme magnificently exemplifies this point: it serves its purpose of signaling "menace" from the first time it is heard, despite its recognizability as film music "menace." (We learn its convention quickly and after that first hearing it signals "shark menace"; see the discussion of "leitmotiv" below.)

Source scoring is the music that falls between diegetic and nondiegetic music. As Hagen puts it:

> This kind of music is like source in its content, but tailored to meet scoring requirements. . . . This kind of cue can start as pure source music and change over to source scoring. . . . The main difference between Source and Source Scoring is that source scoring takes on a much closer relationship to the film. It follows the framework of the scene more critically and matches the nuances of the scene musically. (1971: 190)

Source scoring combines aspects of source music and dramatic scoring in terms of both its relationship to the film's narrative world and its coincidence with the onscreen events.[5] In a sequence in *Dead Again*, composer Patrick Doyle plays on the idea of source scoring. Under hypnosis, Grace (Emma Thompson) realizes that Mike (Kenneth Branagh) is part of the Roman Strauss/Margaret Strauss past. When they return to his apartment, she is frightened by the image of him opening letters with a pair of scissors; meanwhile, Trudy, Mike's downstairs neighbor, practices her scales in a recurring bit of musical business. Mike realizes Grace's fear and becomes angry, dragging her throughout the apartment to collect up every pair of scissors, as Trudy's scales get faster and faster, more and more polished and frantic. As Mike and Grace sit on the bed beginning to calm down, Trudy's scales return to their normal pace, hesitancy, and clumsiness. So, as Hagen describes, what begins as source music matches the narrative events as if it were dramatic scoring. (When Mike inadvertently calls Grace "Margaret," however, full orchestral stinger chords operate at a level of specificity that points out the limits of source scoring. Trudy's scales could never manage the precision of fear and horror that these stingers—sforzando chords to mark dramatic tension—signify.)

Source scoring can also connect characters or events across vast divides of narrative time or space. In one of the final sequences of *Mississippi Masala*, for example, there is a series of cuts from Jay in Uganda to Kinnu, his wife, reading his letter in her store and back to Jay again. Beginning with that first shot of Jay, there is a harmonica blues that must be dramatic scoring. After the cut to Kinnu, however, there is a pan around the store to Skillet, an older black musician, playing the harmonica. The music is thus established as source music in the shot of Kinnu. But on the second cut back to Jay, Skillet's harmonica playing acquires an interstitial status that can only be described as source scoring. Similarly, in *Moonstruck*, Loretta comes home to prepare for her trip to the opera. She turns on the radio to some contemporary light jazz. The music continues over several dissolves that clearly signify time passage, yet the music is not disrupted in any way. What began as music coming from the radio has clearly shifted status, just as Skillet's harmonica blues did.

In some cases, the idea of source scoring may be useful to describe musical events whose narrative status is open to interpretation. For example, in the final sequence of *Star Wars* (during which Princess Leia gives Luke and Han medals), the music can be understood as slipping back and forth between "diegetic" and "nondiegetic." A majestic, somber minor-key march accompanies Luke and Han (and Chewie)'s walk up the aisle, but a much more upbeat, though still majestic, major key accompanies Leia's bestowal of the medals. There are no musicians on screen, and the music is plausible either as part of the ceremony or as dramatic scoring of the scene. Thus, this music occupies an ambiguous position within the narrative world of the film, while retaining a limited but clear relationship to the events of that world.

It is possible to hear the music in this sequence as clearly dramatic scoring, since it includes statements of earlier themes (and since the rebels have not been shown traveling with an orchestra). This music surely is perceived by some as dramatic scoring. For others, however, the presence of an orchestra at such a ceremony at the rebel base is either plausible or *never even questioned*, since ceremonies (graduations, weddings, and other center-aisle marches) have accompanying music, and the status of John Williams's theme in the lives of the rebels is similarly not at issue. The music in this sequence can be either dramatic scoring or source scoring, according to how it is perceived.[6]

The inside/outside, diegetic/nondiegetic dichotomy has difficulty with all of these musical events; they belong to a third "in-between" category. Moreover, it cannot analyze the degree to which music takes cues from other filmic events. Most importantly, it cannot account for the *relationship* between these two qualities. The approach of composers, however, is able to account for questions both of narrativity and of cueing and, by implication, for the relationship of these questions as well: they exist in a kind

Example 1
Star Wars: Closing ceremonial march

of inverse proportionality in which the more identifiably within the narrative the music is produced, the less liable it is to take its cues from the events of the narrative.

Music and the Scene: "Music History" and "Attention" Continua

Parallel with questions of the relationship between the music and the narrative world lie questions concerning the way the music functions in a specific scene. Does the music refer to other music within the film? Outside the film? How much attention does the music demand from the audience? The relationship of film music to other music or other aspects of the film is not sufficiently described by a priori categories. Approaches to these relationships must take into account that films are only partly discrete entities: they exist for perceivers within a web of textuality that includes experiences of sound, music, and visuals that begins long before a specific film experience and continues long thereafter.

The Music History Continuum

As I argued in the previous chapter, people subconsciously acquire sociohistorically specific musical languages that function for them and for those who address them musically. The language of classical Hollywood makes music useful for film, and both the filmmakers and film perceivers call upon it during every film event. In this sense, all music always refers to other music. There are, however, uses of film music that refer directly to other specific musical events. Borrowing from literary and operatic terminology, I call these uses *quotation, allusion,* and *leitmotiv.*

Quotation is the importing of a song or musical text, in part or in whole, into a film's score. Many compiled scores of the 1980s and 1990s build a whole score based on quotations. David Shumway has suggested that the roots of these contemporary compiled scores can be found in early rock scores such as those of *The Graduate* (1967) and *Easy Rider* (1969). Jeff Smith goes back even earlier, to the use of "Rock Around the Clock" in *Blackboard Jungle* (1955). But the phenomenal possibilities were not much exploited until, perhaps, *American Graffiti* (1973) and *Saturday Night Fever* (1977). The compiled score was really institutionalized in the 1980s by *The Big Chill* (1983; see chapters 3 and 5 for discussions of this kind of score). Since then, quotation has become one of the staple forms of music in contemporary scores.

Allusion in a score is a particular kind of quotation, that is, a quotation used to evoke another narrative. The helicopter attack scene in *Apocalypse Now*, during which the attackers blast Wagner's "Ride of the Valkyries," is an example of this, as is the "Dying Swan" in Cassavetes's *A Woman Under the Influence*. One of the most complex (and most talked about) examples of allusive music in a contemporary Hollywood film is the role of *La Bohème* in *Moonstruck*. The works quoted belong to an entire narrative, such as opera or ballet; in a few seconds of film time, an allusion can evoke another whole narrative for the perceiver familiar with the excerpt. While one might argue that the uses of popular musics that I cited above as "quotations" could be allusions to entire genres, I want to retain here the specificity of allusions to preexisting narratives, and thus exclude single songs from this definition unless they belong to a larger narrative work.

Leitmotiv is a Wagnerian term that has become standard in film music criticism.[7] The *Harvard Brief Dictionary of Music* defines it as

> a short theme or musical idea consistently associated with a character, a place or an object, a certain situation or a recurrent idea of the plot. . . . These motifs are used, not as rigidly fixed melodies, but in a very flexible manner. . . . (Appel and Daniel 1960: 56)

In this case, music refers to other musical events within the film as an identifying or cueing mark. Gorbman's extended analysis of motifs in *Mildred Pierce* describes the "classical" use of leitmotiv in film scoring; this kind of score continues to be very common (1987: 93–97). (Some recent examples include John Williams's scores for the Star Wars and Indiana Jones films, Bruce Broughton's for *Young Sherlock Holmes*, and John Morris's for *Dirty Dancing*.) "Foggy Mountain Breakdown" in *Bonnie and Clyde* is a less traditional leitmotiv; it signals to the perceiver an editorial leap in time and space (a scene change). And "Che Gelida Manina," from *La Bohème*, is both an allusion and a leitmotiv as it is used throughout *Moonstruck*.

Not all music refers specifically to music within the film or to other music outside the film. One could perhaps call music that does not refer to other specific music "pure," "unique," "nonreferential," but none of these terms are free of inappropriate and/or misleading connotations. I call this kind of music *one-time music,* meaning simply music that has not been heard before the first viewing of a particular scene, and presumably will not be heard in any other context. On rare occasions, this status is problematized. For example, Earle Hagen's theme to the TV series *Mike Hammer* reappears as the music of a burlesque performance in *Blaze*. I would retain the definition of this as one-time music, although it is clearly possible that some perceivers might remember the theme from *Mike Hammer*, as I did, and therefore experience that music as allusive.

This does not imply that one-time music has no relationship to other music. All music refers to other music. Music in the mainstream of its historical tradition uses established musical codes to convey a mood or idea, and music breaking with its historical tradition refers to that tradition by interrupting the audience's expectations. There is a vast field of musical experience—ranging from background music for film and television to "golden oldies" to "classical" music—that forms our musical heritage in this culture. And it is this common heritage on which both composers and listeners draw for meaning in music, as described in chapter 1. In other words, all music, including film music, exists for the listener on this time, or history, continuum. The *specific* musical event may or may not refer to other *specific* musical events either within or before the film, but in any case will certainly refer to other musical events in order to convey meaning. All musical events signify within an overarching field of music and within a genre or style, employing a set of rules that govern the real or possible musical events that comprise the genre (Fabbri 1982: 52).

The Attention Continuum

The music in a given film scene relates to the narrative world of the film, and to other music; it also interacts with other aspects of the scene. How much attention do viewers/listeners give to the music, in comparison to the dialogue, visuals, and other elements? Again, a highly complex and indeterminate quality is at issue. Attention to music depends on many factors, including the volume of the music, its style, and its "appropriateness" in the scene. The degree of attention given to the music can be anywhere along an infinitely divisible continuum ranging from none to all; rarely, if ever, does an instance of film music belong on either end of the spectrum.

Many factors determine how much attention particular instances of music command, including technology, instrumentation, style, etc. For example, a variety of forms of postproduction manipulations can set parameters of listening. Or, as Jeff Smith describes, a pop score can use a riff or hook to "engage a listener's attention, to 'sell' a song, as it were, by providing a unique and instantly memorable musical idea within the confines of a standardized song form" (1998: 8). Here, however, I am discussing attention as a relationship between music and other components in the scene (action, dialogue, sound effects, etc.).

The theme song, where it exists, is generally given a very high degree of attention. Audience members may be familiar with it before they enter the viewing situation, from radio play, television advertisements, or film trailers. It occurs most often during the main titles and/or establishing sequence of the film, when the film has not yet "absorbed" the audience into the narrative world of the film. (It may, and often does, also appear later in the film, functioning as a kind of leitmotiv.) Even in this case, however, there is a wide range of possibilities, depending on the complexity of visual material—for example, action, editing pace, framing, focal length, and other auditory material—within the scene, and aspects of the music itself. Often, it stands out as a marketing device as well. For example, the media activity around the making and release of a new James Bond film, such as *Tomorrow Never Dies* (1997), often gives as much attention to the "casting" of the singer (in this case Sheryl Crow) as to the casting of the heroine. (Some classical scores are built around a single theme; see Kalinak's discussion of *Laura*, 1992: 159–83.)

The next point to mark on this imaginary continuum is music as the only sound in the scene, in which there is neither dialogue nor sound effects with which it competes for attention. It is no coincidence that Gorbman chooses the bicycling scene from *Jules et Jim* (in which Jules, Jim, and Catherine take a bicycle tour on a country road) on which to perform the "commutation" exercise described earlier in chapter 1. It is memorable precisely because the scene is structured to give a great deal of attention to the music: there is no other soundtrack, and the visual events are limited and repetitive. Kalinak points out that when dramatic scoring is used to provide structural unity across a discontinuous sequence like the montage in *Captain Blood*, synchronized speech and other diegetic sounds are often suspended to ensure the continuity that only the music can provide (80–83). In each case, the absence of anything besides music on the soundtrack serves to focus attention quite specifically onto the music.

Similar to sole-soundtrack music is music with very little competition from other aural or visual material. For example, in a sequence early in *Dangerous Minds*, LouAnn Johnson (Michele Pfeiffer) sits at her desk reading books on teaching techniques and classroom discipline. The score by Wendy and Lisa has a very high audio profile, but is mixed down under one passage when LouAnn reads aloud from a book. When she stops, the music is mixed back up again. Like the sequence Kalinak describes from *Captain Blood*, time passes while the music continues, and we see LouAnn in bed the next morning. There are other sounds on the soundtrack— she throws aside the books, she sits up in her bed—but they are very low profile in comparison to the music.

Further along the continuum are scenes in which there is a great deal of visual action, usually with both sound effects and music, but little or no dialogue. One classic example is the car/subway chase scene in *The French Connection*. The scene is difficult to forget, but the music is not. Similarly, in the sequence in *Dances with Wolves* in which the Pawnee attack the soldiers and facilitate Lt. Dunbar's escape, the continuous music holds together frantically paced editing and subsumes the sounds of bodies dropping into the river and being hit with arrows, gunshots, and so on. In these instances, music often provides a sense of pace and unity without commanding much attention.

Lastly, music commands least attention when it is used as background to dialogue. Composers consider this a particular problem to be handled with great delicacy. When Hagen questioned composers on this issue, he got fairly strong, considered responses:

[Alfred Newman:] I have strong feelings about too much motion and elaborate counterpoint under dialogue. It seems to me that dialogue furnishes rhythm, thus a minimum of orchestral motion is desirable.

[Jerrald Goldsmith:] [Under dialogue,] one must keep music as simple as possible, but while it may sound contradictory, there are times when a certain emotional involvement of the music helps too.

[Quincy Jones:] If it is nonsensical kind of dialogue, there are many cases where you don't have to be as cautious as if it is plot exposition. (1971: 160–61)

The general consensus among composers seems to be that music as background to dialogue should be simple, subtle, and soft, but that the possibilities depend to a large extent on the importance of the dialogue to the film. For example, in the sequence in *Death in Venice* in which Aschenbach first sees Tadzio, the source music figures much more prominently on the soundtrack than does the dialogue. More typically, the score of *Dances with Wolves* always carefully leaves room—in terms of pitch, timbre, and volume—for Kevin Costner's voiceovers. Even the sequences of Lakota conversation, in which understanding the dialogue for the vast majority of viewers is a matter of reading subtitles, are carefully scored not to compete or interfere with the spoken voices.

In each specific case, the rest of the soundtrack and other aspects of the film define the limits of the music's prominence; the mixed-down dialogue (as well as the extended takes and long shooting) in the above-mentioned *Death in Venice* sequence raises the lower limit of attention to the music. Attention will vary from perceiver to perceiver, but these limits define the range of possibilities available to perceivers in making meaning of the music and its functions.

Music and the Message: When, Where, Who, What?

Finally, the question of what the music evokes demands attention. This question has already been discussed at length in chapter 1, and suggested as well at several earlier points. It is arguably the most complex and murky. For different perceivers specific music will evoke different things. As Leonard B. Meyer argues,

> Even where the original association appears to be relevant and appropriate to the character of the music being played, affective experience may be a result of the private meaning that the image has for the particular listener. For example, the image of a triumphal procession might within a given culture be relevant to the character of a piece of music; but the association might for private reasons arouse feelings of humiliation or defeat. Thus while the image itself is relevant to the music, the significance that it has for the particular individual is purely personal. (1956: 257)

Further complicating Meyer's model of cultural or personal meaning are subcultural musical practices and genres. But we can at least begin by considering the usual or dominant meanings of any example of film music.

Film music serves three broad purposes: *identification, mood,* and *commentary.* In one sense, all (or almost all) music in narrative film functions to create mood; here, I am using the term *mood music* specifically to refer to music that is similar in emotional tone to other threads of the film. Music used for identification (or reference) does not preclude the same music simultaneously being used for mood or commentary, although the latter two uses are less frequently combined.

Identifying music can convey or evoke all of the things mentioned in the definition of leitmotiv—"a character, a place or an object, a certain situation, or a recurrent idea of the plot"—as well as period, time, depth of field, and certain sociological factors. Characters and ideas are often identified musically by use of a leitmotiv, although there are numerous exceptions, based mainly on types. The entrance of a villain or hero in an action film, for example, can be prepared by "one-time" music of a type perceivers recognize not only within the film, but also as a standard type of music. In fact, all leitmotivs are first perceived as one-time music; it is only when the same motive appears in relation to the same character or idea that it begins to accumulate a more specific meaning. In other words, to return to the *Jaws* example, the first entry of the theme signifies danger; thereafter, the theme signifies the danger of the shark specifically. Similarly, Darth Vader's theme in *The Empire Strikes Back* signifies "villain" from its first appearance, long before it comes to be associated specifically with Lord Vader. In fact, it appears in the score before Vader appears visually on the screen. (See Kalinak 1992: 194–98 for a discussion of this theme.)

Identifying music often marks other features of a film as well. For instance, setting is often identified by quoted source music. *American Graffiti* signals that it is a period piece in part by the use of period music on radios. *Saturday Night Fever* uses the music as one marker of the setting both in time and in the social structure; disco was a popular music contemporaneous with the film's production (1977) and probably signaled working-class position (and perhaps something about ethnicity) in the imagination of white middle-class perceivers. (It would probably not signal either "class" or "ethnicity" to its regular consumers, but rather something like "my group.")

A more recent, and in many ways more complicated, use of music for similar purposes is *I Like It Like That*, a romantic comedy about Latina/o New York. Its music marks out both community and class for perceivers unfamiliar with contemporary Latin music in North America. For its own community, it makes clear generational distinctions between salsa and merengue and rap; in fact, two volumes of the soundtrack album were released concentrating partly on these two different generations of music.

"One-time" dramatic scoring serves composers as a common tactic for signaling or reinforcing "exotic" geographic locations: "If we see a picture shot in China, we immediately have the fourths and gongs going" (Goldsmith, as quoted in Hagen 1971: 165). It is important to remember here that the music signifies ethnicity (as all other qualities) within our particular musical heritage, not simply by borrowing directly from the culture it attempts to evoke. As Goldsmith remarks: "What is ethnic is what Hollywood has made ethnic. . . . The ethnic-Oriental is particularly worth talking about because if one were to give the pure ethnological answer musically, they [the director and producer?] would throw it out in a second" (Hagen 1971: 164). For example, the first shots of *Indiana Jones and the Temple of Doom* are of a large bare-chested Asian man striking an enormous gong and then a pair of ivory dragons clouded by smoke. The score here is standard Hollywood orchestral fare, and it continues under Kate Capshaw's entrance. But when she steps in front of the title of the film, there is a stereotypical Chinese music figure.

In this way, perceivers are addressed as members of the dominant musical culture; Hollywood's ideas of Chinese music undoubtedly signify differently to Chinese perceivers than they do to white U.S. perceivers.

Mood is at once the most obvious and the most difficult to analyze of all film music's messages. It is frequently expressed by one-time dramatic scoring. While it is mainly simple enough to describe the mood being expressed by an instance of music, the very notion of mood music raises a difficult question: *whose* mood is being expressed? It may be a character in the scene, a character in the film but not in the scene (and who may or may not enter after the music has already begun), or another subjectivity altogether.

Music signifying mood and identification at the same time is quite common, especially in theme songs. For example, in the "wide-open spaces" themes of westerns, perceivers are likely to hear both "old west frontier" and the freedom often associated with it. The theme to *Star Trek: Deep Space Nine* signifies a space station by identifying the place, space, through its instrumentation, and the mood, stasis, through its harmonic procedures.

Finally, there exists the possibility of music used as commentary, countermood, or *Verfremdungseffekt*.[8] *Commentary music*, for example, might tell us that a seemingly romantic situation is actually humorous, or that the daisy-filled meadow contains some unseen danger, or it might break or prevent suture (prevent us from becoming "absorbed" in the film). In this sense, one might argue that "mood" and "commentary" are versions of the same attribute, or different "quantities" of the same "quality." I believe, however, that this would make aspects of their functions less clear, insofar as mood is more often associated with (unconscious) identification processes, while commentary often requests reflective evaluation. Horror music, as a common case of commentary, clarifies this problem. While most film perceivers seem to recognize horror music on a conscious level, it also does its unconscious mood work simultaneously. The signification "danger" is understood consciously—the commentary function—while the unconscious increase in tension (leading to terror) is experienced—the mood function. To return one last time to the *Jaws* theme, then, we can see how mood, commentary, and identification can all overlap; this theme is most often mood, commentary, *and* identification sole-soundtrack leitmotiv dramatic scoring.

Moreover, the problem of the "conscious"/"unconscious" distinction and simultaneity returns us to the "attention" continuum. It might seem that this continuum could be expressed in
terms of degree of *conscious* attention, but the above consideration
of horror music should make the problems with this clear. On the
other hand, it is less likely, as a broad generality, that perceivers
will pay as much attention to mood music as to commentary, or
(from the reverse perspective) that, for example, sole-soundtrack
music will be perceived as subconsciously as music under dialogue.

A Preliminary Vocabulary for Film Music Analysis

In separating the issues discussed in the sections "Music and the
Narrative," "Music and the Scene," and "Music and the Message,"
I tried not to encourage the kind of analytical method I avoided
throughout this chapter. None of these issues exists separately
from any other, but they must be recognized before their relationships can be analyzed. It is important to note that in the analysis of any specific film music, treating one of these issues is likely
to be misleading without also considering the others and the relationships among them. I have indicated within the chapter what
an analysis of these relationships might look like, using terms from
earlier sections to point out common (clichéd?) alignments such
as "ethnic one-time dramatic scoring." These common alignments
remain among the many underanalyzed aspects of film music.

Establishing that film music is a semiotic system both in its own
right and within films only makes possible the process of analyzing the dispersed identification processes within which it operates. Film music conditions identification processes in powerful
ways. Throughout the second section of this study, I will argue
that analyses of those identification processes provide a new realm
of possibilities for both film theory and the study of music.

3

A Woman Scored

During the 1980s, the number of films scored with popular music soundtracks rose dramatically. Films from a wide range of genres appeared with pop soundtracks of various kinds. The success of the soundtrack album of *The Big Chill* created a craze for compiled scores, that is, soundtracks that are a compilation of (usually rock and pop) songs, while growing numbers of MIDI-literate musicians offered the possibility of synthesized scores at very attractive prices. These trends provoke many different kinds of questions for both producers and scholars. What kinds of pop scores are most common? Which films (or groups or genres of films) tend to have popular music scores? What meanings do pop scores bring to films? What meanings might audiences make of them?

These questions take on a particular shape in compiled popular music scores for films centering on female characters. After marking some founding "deaf spots" in popular music studies and feminist film theory, I discuss the scores of several such films that do not use classical Hollywood scoring. They suggest that compiled scores, at least, require new approaches that stage productive critiques of both popular music studies and feminist film theory.

Returning Desire and Agency:
Simon Frith and Teresa de Lauretis

Much work in popular music studies takes place on the terrain of Marxist approaches to popular culture. As Keith Negus writes in his introductory popular music studies textbook,

> In chapter 1 I start by considering how different writers have characterized the audiences for popular music (which in recent times has frequently been as active, creative and oppositional) and then provide an immediate contrast to this in chapter 2 by focusing on approaches to the music industry (often portrayed as mechanistic, exploitative and conservative). These first two chapters are set up in this way so as to emphasize a series of dichotomies that have often separated discussions of musical production and consumption (commerce/creativity, determinism/free will, constraining/liberating). . . . (1996: 2)

Such oppositions have long haunted much work in popular music studies. As early as *Sound Effects* (1981), Simon Frith identified the conflict and worked through both positions; nearly twenty years later, the question persists.

Early feminist film theory had to contend with a similar theoretical sticking point, although it appears at first glance to be radically different. Psychoanalytic film theory focused on what it called "spectatorship" or "spectator positionality," textually produced subject positions from which a film can be read. This spectatorship involved an elaborate series of mechanisms, all deployed in ways that made the film the endpoint of the camera's gaze, and the protagonist—and by a series of transferences, the director and the spectator—its beginning. When Laura Mulvey pointed out in 1975 that these models of film spectatorship were inherently (that is, both theoretically and filmically) gendered, feminist theorists of film began a long struggle to describe feminine spectator positions and to account for identification processes available to women/female spectators.

Since that model of feminist film theory consistently worked from derivations of structuralist models of psychic processes (Lacan), narrative (Genette, Lotman), and language (Saussure), inquiry was mainly directed toward texts. Questions of either production and industries or consumption and audiences disappeared in discussions of how traditional editing practices and camera technique created suture and spectator positions. At worst, "readers" functioned only as spaces for the cultural product to do its work.

In "Desire in Narrative" (1984), a crucial early attempt to introduce the social into psychoanalytic theories, Teresa de Lauretis described identification processes that significantly resemble the oppression/liberation problem in popular music studies. She argued that there are two distinct kinds of relays that produce identification, one based on looking and seeing, the other on narrative. Visual identification, when considered without narrativity, might relegate the "woman spectator" to the entirely masculine position Mulvey first articulated. But, de Lauretis argued, narrative identification offers two different positions—"the figure of narrative movement, the mythical subject, and ... the figure of narrative closure, the narrative image" (1984: 144). In other words, a narrative has one and only one agent, and that agent is a male figure (the figure of narrative movement). As I described in chapter 1, de Lauretis built this argument on Jurij Lotman's plot typology, in which he says that there are only two types of characters—mobile heroes and immobile figures of plot space—and two motions—entry into and exit from closed space. De Lauretis aligned immobile figures of plot space with "non-man, an absolute abstraction" (p. 121), and further with the narrative image, the figure of narrative closure.

Through analysis of these two figures, she argued that narrative identification is *always* double;

> both figures can and in fact must be identified with at once, for they are inherent in narrativity itself. It is this narrative identification that assures "the hold of the image," the anchoring of the subject in the flow of the film's movement; rather than, as Metz proposes, the primary identification with the all-perceiving subject of the gaze. (p. 144)

The coproduction of narrativity and spectatorship she posited connects the pair narrative movement/narrative image to seeing/seen. In terms of the deployment of power, these founding oppositions of feminist film theories and of Marxist popular culture studies—liberatory/oppressive, seeing/seen, narrative movement/narrative closure—are structurally identical and epistemologically similar. And de Lauretis's answer is quite similar to Frith's; each rejects the either/or option in favor of both/and. In terms of their relations to agency on the one hand and desire on the other, however, their differences demand close attention.

Theories of identification processes have still not adequately engaged questions of agency. Their concern has been with the structures and operations of desire and fantasy. But the consequence of these structuralist tendencies in psychoanalysis has been its undoing. Many feminist theorists have abandoned it altogether in favor of, for example, empirical audience studies, not least because psychoanalytic theory's "stiffness" makes it difficult to talk about differences among women, or differences in identification processes, along lines other than gender or sexual difference.

On the other hand, Marxist theories of popular culture provide no model for describing engagements between desire and texts. While "false consciousness" has long been critiqued as demeaning and overly simple, a dedication to agency and intentionality has prevailed in popular music studies, preventing it from considering subjectivity as a major theoretical issue. It is, for instance, telling that one of the earliest and only articles in popular music studies that engages film and literary studies' debates about subjectivity, Sean Cubitt's "Maybellene: Meaning and the Listening Subject" (1984), is rarely cited and has not yet provoked a similar debate in popular music studies. Similarly, David Schwarz's article "Listening Subjectivity" ([1993] 1997a) on new minimal music has not been taken up by music theory or musicologists. "Listening" has never come close to having the same intellectual force as "reading" in literary studies and "spectatorship" in film studies.

The similarity between Negus's description and the questions Simon Frith poses at the end of the second chapter of *Sound Effects* indicates the degree to which the opposition capitalist/oppressive versus populist/popular/liberatory still governs popular music studies. Frith says:

> The problematic issue that runs (if in different ways) through the history of all forms of popular music since the development of industrial capitalism is the relationship between music as a means of popular expression and music as a means of making money.... [R]ock fun is never really "innocent"—there are always manipulative processes involved; but neither is rock consumption necessarily therefore "passive"—rock meanings aren't *determined* by their commercial means of production. (1981: 38)

Throughout the book, Frith attempts to maintain both positions simultaneously, but instead oscillates between them. The organization of the book itself contributes to producing this theoretical problem: the sections are called "Rock Meanings," "Rock Production," and "Rock Consumption," suggesting that separating these issues breaks them down into manageable "chunks." It does, of course, but the separation also makes it difficult to trace the coproduction and comanagement of meaning, production, and pleasure. The problem of *Sound Effects* may be grounded in the difficulty of trying to think about rock music in circulation (through production, text, reading, and lived cultures) by thinking of it as a series of moments.

In the last two paragraphs of the book—a section entitled "Last Words"—Frith faces the oscillation again:

> Rock music is capitalist music. It draws its meanings from the relationships of capitalist production, and it contributes, as a leisure activity, to the reproduction of those relationships; the music doesn't challenge the system but reflects and illuminates it. Rock is about dreams and their regulation, and the strength of rock dreams comes not from their force as symbols, but from their relationship to the experience of work and leisure: the issue, finally, is not how to live outside capitalism (hippie or bohemian style), but how to live within it. The needs expressed in rock—for freedom, control, power, a sense of *life*—are needs defined by capitalism. And rock is a mass culture. It is not folk or art but a commoditized dream: it conceals as much as it reveals. For every individual illuminating account of our common situation there are a hundred mass musical experiences that disguise it. Rock, for all the power of its individual dreams, is still confined by its mass cultural form. Its history, like the history of America itself, is a history of class struggle—the struggle for fun. (pp. 271–72)

Frith locates rock, quite rightly, in terms of its relationship to capitalism, and in this all popular music theorists agree. What I find compelling about his description here is its proximity to the issues of subjectivity and psychoanalytic models so rigorously denied by popular music studies. To say that the needs expressed in rock are the needs defined by capitalism is, I think, to say with Althusser that we are subjects formed in ideology. To call rock a commoditized dream is to say that it is not only about the commodity but also about desire and fantasy, a never-to-be-fulfilled desire tapped by musical as well as verbal and visual signifying systems for processes of identification. This implied subjectivity, which never enters Frith's theoretical account, never has the chance to mediate the disturbingly unsettled waters as was promised earlier on. Nor has it entered popular music studies since; its absence is a constitutive deaf spot of the field.

De Lauretis has a similar problem in "Desire in Narrative." She states emphatically that the double narrative identifications are simultaneous:

> The analogy that links identification-with-the-look to masculinity and identification-with-the-image to femininity breaks down precisely when we think of a spectator alternating between the two. Neither can be abandoned for the other, even for a moment; no image can be identified, or identified with, apart from the look that inscribes it as image, and vice versa. (pp. 142–43)

She associates the failure to understand this simultaneity with the absence of sexual difference as a category in earlier psychoanalytic film theories, and with Mulvey's ascription of a "purely" masculine position to cinematic identification. Somewhat later, however, when attempting to articulate a position that could be called "resistant spectatorship" (it remains unnamed in her text), she says:

... if the spectator's identification is engaged and directed in each film by specific cinematic-narrative codes (the place of the look, the figures of narrative), it should be possible to work through those codes in order to shift or redirect identification toward the two positionalities of desire that define the female's Oedipal situation; and if the alternation between them is protracted long enough (as has been said of *Rebecca*) or in enough films (and several have already been made), the viewer may come to suspect that such duplicity, such contradiction cannot and perhaps even need not be resolved. (p. 153)

The alternation that produced a theoretical failure a few pages earlier now becomes the marker of a feminist future for film. Like Frith, de Lauretis uses a sleight-of-hand to introduce agency by implying a progressive feminist future based on authorial intent— that is, good feminist filmmakers making good feminist films would change the conditions and interplays of subjectivity, desire, and identification for their viewers. Annette Kuhn and many feminist film theorists proposed quite similar programs, and "reading against the grain" became a dominant paradigm of feminist film studies. While it may be troubling to locate all power once again in production-text relations, it seems clear that de Lauretis's proposal at least reintroduces agency and consciousness into psychoanalytic theory. And while film studies struggles with the legacy of these questions, it has by no means found its way to a compelling account of agency.

I have combed through Frith's and de Lauretis's texts so carefully to show both that the "repressed" of the unconscious returns in Marxist approaches, and that agency cannot be silenced in psychoanalysis. And while these texts—from twenty years ago— articulate early positions in popular music studies and feminist film theory as we now know them, these repressions have not changed. Neither studies of identification processes with film nor popular music scholarship have reconciled the conflicts of desire and agency. But at least in the case of popular music sound-tracks—as I discuss in the next section—both are necessary to any understanding of film music identification processes.

Singing a Song of Sexuality:
Cay, Vivian, Brenda, Jasmin, Baby, Johnny,
Thelma and Louise

In film after film since the mid-1980s, scores for female narrative agents have abandoned the symphonic Romanticism of classical Hollywood in favor of pop—and especially compiled—sound-tracks.[1] Surely, a major factor in the trend toward pop scoring is soundtrack album sales, but just as surely, that is insufficient explanation for the particularly widespread use of compiled scores in films with "updated" female characters. In classical Hollywood film, female characters are traditionally defined by the two sexu-alities Kalinak describes in "The Fallen Woman and the Virtuous Wife" (1982). And agents of narrative are male. Thus, films with female narrative agents themselves take on the embattled rela-tionship between desire and agency by representing agency in female characters and by putting them at the center of their nar-ratives. This contradiction has drawn feminist film analysts for some time. Combined with film studies' penchant for classical Hollywood films as objects of study, the conflict between desire and agency made film noir and "weepies" the major genres of feminist film theorizing in the 1970s and 1980s (for example, Kaplan 1978; Doane 1987; Gledhill 1987; Flinn 1992).

The relationship between desire and agency in the films consid-ered in this chapter is enacted in particular ways by their pop scores, ways that point to the problems these scores manifest for the dominant theoretical paradigms of both popular culture studies and feminist film theory. Pop soundtracks highlight the deaf spots of both feminist film theories and popular music studies because popular musics depend on a web of memory, emotion, and identification—that is, on the mutual predication of desire and agency. The soundtracks point toward a Marxist psychoanalysis in which desire and agency would not only not be radically separated, but would be analyzed as mutually defining and producing.

Of the five films considered in this chapter, *Dangerous Liaisons* is the only one that does not use popular music in its soundtrack. Most of its score consists of Baroque period music, whose obvious function is to signify historical location, much like period costumes and sets. To leave analysis of the soundtrack there, however, dismisses some of its most unusual features. There are a number of reasons to suspect that the Baroque score activates more meanings than simply period. For example, one of the few instances of traditional Hollywood scoring is used for a sexual scene between the Vicomte de Valmont (John Malkovich) and Madame de Tourvel (Michele Pfeiffer). As Valmont pushes Tourvel down on the bed, kissing her, the music suddenly swells in lush romantic language. The movie's ending, in which we discover that Valmont and Tourvel truly loved each other, comes as no surprise to the film's soundtrack, because it knew there was "real" emotion between them much earlier.

But, as I argued in the first chapter, the possibilities for female characters in classical Hollywood scoring are severely limited. Scoring the Marquise de Merteuil (Glenn Close) as one of classical Hollywood's two options—a fallen woman or a virtuous wife—would significantly change the film. Baroque music has a potentially contradictory range of connotations, including intricacy, excess, ornamentation, restraint, calculation, and lack of emotion. These qualities describe the film's vision of the Marquise far more accurately than a jazz sax could—while both the sax and the harpsichord can convey the strategic deployment of a female body in service of acquiring power, the Marquise's particular *kind* of power is not within the repertoire of classical Hollywood's ideas about female sexuality.

The associations of Baroque music, by themselves, are too diffuse to serve *Dangerous Liaison*'s purposes. The opening sequence of the film narrows its meaning in the film's internal language; Baroque music, within the film, means dry, unemotional calculation. For the first three minutes, shots alternate between the Marquise and Valmont, each being groomed and dressed by a host of servants, choosing wigs and shoes and earrings, being powdered and sewn into clothing, taking on the trappings they require to function for a day. These activities, the background music, and the camera work join to make this establishing sequence exude a calculated and elaborate production of self and power.

And it is in part the use of Baroque music through which the film positions the Marquise as its central figure. The effect of the very final sequence of the film—in which we see the Marquise in a close-up shot, removing her makeup, looking much older, and shedding a single tear—depends on the narrative and musical construction of her as calculating, and that construction depends partly on the meaning of Baroque music within the film. Certainly, this sketch of a reading raises as many questions as it answers, beginning (for example) with why the kinds of power and the kind of female sexuality that the Marquise represents seem to belong in the eighteenth century, and how Baroque music came to acquire the associations it has. But it does show that late German Romanticism is not the only western art music tradition that can be used to score a Hollywood film. And that musics outside classical Hollywood's semiotic code offer a wider range of possibilities for female characters.

For perceivers of *Dangerous Liaisons*, the female narrative agent is made possible because the film created an internal musical language for itself outside of the conventions of classical Hollywood Romanticism. But films with contemporary popular scores and films like *Dangerous Liaisons* with art music scores depend differently on audiences' relationships to their musical genres. I raise the example of an art music score here to point out that pop scores are not the only alternative to classical Hollywood, even if they are currently the most common (and most lucrative, Pachelbel's "Canon" in *Ordinary People* and Ravel's "Bolero" in *10* notwithstanding).

The four films I discuss more fully range from quite small to lavish. *Desert Hearts* is a small independent film that played art houses for short runs and received more attention on video. (It did have selected mainstream release outside the United States, for example, in London.) *Bagdad Cafe* is Percy Adlon's second film, a German independent made-for-TV production with small but worldwide release. *Dirty Dancing* enjoyed the most mainstream success. It was extremely successful as a first-run release, had huge soundtrack and video sales, and even produced a spin-off road company show and concert video. *Thelma and Louise* was something of a sleeper. Audiences, especially women, flocked to it in spite of the bad reviews, and it developed a cult following, with women wearing buttons like "Graduate of the Thelma and Louise Finishing School."[2] These films don't immediately appear to have much in common. But all of them revolve around female narrative agents, and all use popular music scores.

Desert Hearts is the story of two women who fall in love with each other. Cay is an aspiring artist trapped in Reno, the local wild woman "dyke." Vivian is a carefully controlled English professor from Columbia, in Nevada to divorce. The film is based on the 1964 novel by Jane Rule, and is quite well known in lesbian communities. It uses nineteen different country and western and rock 'n' roll songs in its score.[3] These songs are important in the score not because country and western has a precise, guaranteed meaning, but rather because they do not belong to the tight meaning system of classical Hollywood scoring practice. Instead, each of us brings meanings from the individual and collective uses of songs in our everyday lives. The meanings perceivers bring to the songs include some ways that rock 'n' roll or country and western signify as genres, but they also include more specific meanings generated by perceivers' very different relationships to the genres in general as well as the specific songs. Those particular relationships between perceivers and songs help listeners identify with the lovers through our own memories of learning about our sexualities.

The choice of popular musics thus helps make *Desert Hearts* something other than an archetypal Hollywood romance. It avoids the trap of trying to represent lesbian sexualities in terms of Hollywood heterosexist feminine sexuality. By bringing memories, with their associated emotions, from audience members' unconsciouses into consciousness, it both particularizes Cay and Vivian's relationship and provides particularizable paths of entry for identification. And, since Patsy Cline—two of whose songs are used in the film—has a wide following in gay and lesbian communities, it manages to address two distinct audiences—heterosexual and lesbian—along different lines at the same time.[4]

There are, however, indications that *Desert Hearts* is not especially concerned with addressing itself to a heterosexist audience. The scene in which Cay and Vivian first make love has no background music. The soundtrack is filled only with diegetic sound—the sounds produced by their mouths and breath. Since this sequence would traditionally be heavily scored, the absence of music makes it seem more graphic than it actually is. If this scene is addressed to an audience unaccustomed to seeing, or unprepared to see, women making love to each other, it is only by virtue of its shock

value, which could have been reduced drastically had the scene
been scored.[5]

The final sequence of the film, in which Vivian convinces Cay
to ride with her on the train to the next station, uses Ella
Fitzgerald's "I Wished on the Moon." This choice lies outside not
only classical Hollywood scoring practices, but also the genres
established by the rest of the score as its internal language. The rest
of the film's score serves a broad range of purposes, from establishing time and place to addressing different audiences. But jazz
isn't quite so located, especially not this song.[6] The choice of an
Ella tune for the final sequence makes the scene seem somewhat
transcendent, as if it could be taking place anywhere and any-
when, as long as that place and time were not a Hollywood movie.
It also leans the (non)resolution of the film somewhat toward a
happy ending; the urban associations of jazz lend credibility to
the reading that Cay continues on with Vivian to New York.

Like *Desert Hearts*, *Bagdad Cafe* presents an alternative to heterosexual love, but this time it is through an intimate friendship
between the two central characters: Brenda (CCH Pounder), an
African-American owner of a cafe and motel, and Jasmin
(Marianne Sägebrecht), a white German tourist. The film opens
with Jasmin leaving her husband in the middle of the Nevada
desert, and Brenda and her husband getting into a screaming
match that provokes him into leaving her. The film chronicles
the development of their friendship, from mutual terror through
cautious understanding to a centrality ordinarily only granted in
films to heterosexual romantic relationships.

The score's two themes underline the private and public aspects
of their connection; privately, they provide each other with primary companionship, while publicly their relationship magically
transforms the community of the cafe. The interiority of their relationship is the pop ballad "I Am Calling You" (since used in AT&T

Example 2
Bagdad Cafe: Rag

commercials); the magic that their friendship works on the denizens of the Bagdad Cafe is scored with a kind of neo–Scott Joplin rag.

The first theme, including its lyrics, suggests that Brenda and Jasmin's friendship successfully provides the intimacy that their marriages didn't; the second theme suggests that their relationship magically transforms the community around them. The rag theme signifies as a genre, carrying meaning in much the same way that Baroque music does in *Dangerous Liaisons*; "I Am Calling You" functions more in the modality of Patsy Cline in *Desert Hearts,* connecting the friendship with a realm of desire within the audience members' experiences. The rag theme signifies as a piece of music from a historically black genre that became popular internationally and that was repopularized by *The Sting* in 1973. In that way, its bright, cheerful (interracial) sound serves perfectly to represent the black, Native American, and white community of the cafe.

The legato phrasing, the long durations of "I" and "you," and the close-to-the-mike vocal technique all mark the first theme as a love song. It thus enables *Bagdad Cafe*'s audience to imagine female friendships in eroticized terms. Ultimately, each woman repartners—Brenda with Sal and Jasmin with the painter Rudi Cox (Jack Palance). It is, of course, possible to read this as a containment of a lesbian subtext. But the music—both the persistence of "I Am Calling You" and the ending of the film with the rag—suggests instead that Jasmin and Brenda's friendship exceeds any such narrative containment.

Dirty Dancing presents the most conventional sexuality of these four films. (Not coincidentally, it was the most expensive and commercially successful among them.) It uses a combination of period songs, contemporary popular songs, and classical Hollywood techniques to score a film set in 1963. The reason for this choice seems clear enough: *Dirty Dancing* is a teen film, pitched to a teen audience to whom the music of the early 1960s would not necessarily speak. Like that of *Good Morning, Vietnam* or *Dangerous Liaisons* or *American Graffiti,* the soundtrack of *Dirty Dancing* places its auditors in the period in which it is set. But it is also a time-shifting mirror image of *The Big Chill,* which uses older music for the soundtrack of a contemporarily set film to help audience members identify with their peer group as it is being represented on screen. In other words, just as *The Big Chill* uses yesterday's music in a today-set film to connect today's adults with their youth, so *Dirty Dancing* uses today's music in a yesterday-set film to connect today's youth with yesterday's youth. And, by using classical techniques at select moments, it sets firmer boundaries on interpretation than a strictly compiled score could.

The plot of the movie is quite simple: a young girl named Baby, on vacation with her upper-middle-class family, meets a young man—Johnny—working at the resort as a dance instructor. They fall in love, and he teaches her to dance. The characters, too, are familiar: she, a warm-hearted liberal do-gooder; he, a working-class angry (and very sexy) young man. She teaches him about optimism and self-reliance; he teaches her about her body.

The opening sequence establishes the meaning of white sixties music in the film: it is innocent, nostalgic, hearkening back to a prepubescent peace of mind. Baby's family is on their way to a Catskills resort for a vacation. In a voiceover, Baby says:

> That was the summer of 1963, when everybody called me Baby, and it didn't occur to me to mind. That was before President Kennedy was shot, before the Beatles came, when I couldn't wait to join the Peace Corps, and I thought I'd never find a guy as great as my dad.

The song on the radio is "Big Girls Don't Cry." The audio track in this sequence sets up the entire film: Baby is going to learn to mind being called Baby, she is going to find a guy as great as her dad (maybe greater), and liberal politics will have something to do with her accession to adulthood. (One way to read *Dirty Dancing* would be as a female oedipal drama, a reading that this voiceover encourages.)

Music and dance, inseparable throughout the film, define two constellations of identity: middle-aged, middle-class, repressed, and Jewish versus young, working-class, sexual, and not-quite-white (Irish? Italian? Latina/o?). While the guests take mambo and cha-cha dance lessons, the entertainment staff has steamy dances of their own after hours. As Shumway says, "*Dirty Dancing* portrays the R&B records played by its working-class characters as sexually liberating and as transgressive of the aesthetic and moral norms of the middle-class adult culture of the Catskills resort" (1999: 46). In this way, Johnny has—and imparts to Baby—a kind of knowledge from which good daughters of the middle class ought to be protected, at least according to their fathers. (A comparison to *Flashdance* might suggest why female characters can marry up in class, while this is forbidden to male characters.) In the final sequence, when Johnny and Baby dance on stage, her father gets up to stop her, but her mother stops him. She later leans over to her husband and says, "She gets that from me," taking credit for a knowledge of bodies and sexuality that he has tried to deny throughout the movie. (There is an interesting connection between the father's discomfort with bodies and his professional status as a doctor. While bodies are his business, they apparently cannot be his pleasure.)

This final sequence, which contains one of three original songs, quite clearly sets out to connect (and, judging by the reaction of my students at the time, succeeded in connecting) its teen audience with the happenings on stage. They can identify with the heroic gesture Johnny makes in declaring his love for Baby, and they can identify with Baby's rush of romantic pleasure in being so chosen. This worked, in part, because at the time of the film's release "The Time of My Life" was getting lots of airplay. The song was already available to teen audiences for romantic identifications, and the song and the film cross-marketed each other. (Eventually, the road show and the concert video did the same for both the album and the video in an elaborate marketing web.)

The title "The Time of My Life" marks one of the most compelling features of popular music: songs choreograph good and bad times, serving as cues for memories of *specific* times of your life. In other words, the song articulates lyrically one important relationship between popular musics and lived cultures: most people, myself included, organize and evoke their memories in part through practices of music consumption. By combining period songs, such as the Ronette's "Be My Baby" and Otis Redding's "Love Man," with contemporary pop, *Dirty Dancing*'s score was able to agglomerate nostalgia, current top 10 sounds, and classical Hollywood music. In this way, the identifications it conditioned opened onto perceivers' relationships to the songs, but carefully tracked their attachments toward the coming-of-age scenario.

The score of *Thelma and Louise* is also a compiled-composed combination. Country, blues, and rock tunes make up most of the score, with composed synth-blues-rock material for the dramatic sequences. The music is laid down in very nontraditional ways; for example, the second cue in the film (Martha Reeves singing Van Morrison's "Wild Night") begins as Louise walks to her car, not before or on the cut, and not under any sound effect. The combination of vocal music—to which perceivers are likely to give more attention than instrumental music—and nonstandard cueing gives the music an unusually high profile. And the audio mix also makes a high profile on the soundtrack likely. Many songs throughout the film are used as dramatic scoring, and they increase and decrease in volume to allow for dialogue. For example, the third song, "House of Hope," begins as Thelma throws her suitcase in the car, continues over various cuts that signify time passing, and gets softer while Thelma and Louise talk and louder when they've finished. Because quotations of popular songs are less frequently mixed this way—this mixing is usually reserved for one-time dramatic scoring—the rise and fall in volume makes the songs more noticeable. Finally, the mixing makes it possible to hear the lyrics of the songs most of the time, and the lyrics very often contribute to the production of meaning in a sequence.

In this sense, audio production choices condition paths of identification because they condition the attention continuum, just as perceivers' histories condition the music history continuum. Similarly, the relations between music and visual tracks also condition identification processes. Pop song cues match visual tracks quite easily at their entrances, but very rarely do they continue to match tightly. While such sequences could, for example, use music-video-style rhythmic visual editing, or could structure a sequence precisely to follow musical structure or lyrics, such breaks with continuity editing are rarely permitted. Because continuity editing is so inviolable, pop soundtracks have an aleatory quality—the songs have only a very loose fit with the visuals. These loose matches contribute further to the larger range of identifications possible with pop soundtracks than with classical scores.

The early portion of the soundtrack seems to speak for Thelma and Louise differently from the songs in any other film I've discussed so far. While only six of the eighteen songs on the soundtrack are sung by women, four of those comprise the soundtrack until Thelma and Louise arrive at the bar. The soundtrack suggests a world of women that is supported by the visuals and dialogue. The only men in this part of the film are Thelma's husband Darryl, who is irredeemably stupid (later in the film he stands in his pizza), and a cook at the diner who propositions Thelma when she calls to talk to Louise (he has no other lines, and seems like a stereotypical "good ole' boy").

This unlikely space that the film first defines is disrupted by Harlan. When Harlan and Thelma begin to dance, the male vocalist's presence is undeniable—we see the band. For the first time in the film, both musically and visually, Louise and Thelma are represented in relation to the world around them, not just to each other. When they stop after fleeing the parking lot, the song on the coffee shop jukebox is Tammy Wynette's "I Don't Wanna Play House."

It would be difficult not to read this as speaking directly for both Louise and Thelma. As the movie continues, it becomes clear that Thelma will not play house with Darryl any more, and Louise won't start doing it with Jimmy. (In fact, they have so completely rejected being relegated to domestic space that they never again enter it. We see Darryl in his house, and Detective Slocum breaking into Louise's apartment, and Jimmy in his apartment, but never again does either Thelma or Louise enter a home or apartment.) But even as early as this coffee shop sequence, the music clearly suggests that they have begun to reject traditional gendered power dynamics.[7]

By using popular music, the film grounds the entire narrative in the everyday. The apparently fantastic story of two women shooting some guy in a parking lot, taking off, holding up convenience stores and blowing up big rigs becomes more "natural" when the music that accompanies it sounds like what one listens to in one's own car rather than in a symphony concert hall.[8] (In this way, it becomes immediately apparent how socially conditioned this kind of audio identification process is. Some people's car radios routinely emit country music like that of Charlie Sexton and Grayson Hugh, others are tuned in to rock 'n' roll oldies, and many are unlikely ever to hear a single song from the soundtrack of *Thelma and Louise* in an everyday context.) Part of our access to identification with Thelma and Louise depends on our access to identification with their music, which helps explain the peculiar combination of, for example, Tammy Wynette, B. B. King, and Michael McDonald (of the Doobie Brothers). Processes of audio identification—which are crucial to the operation of this film—are facilitated by the presence of country, blues, and rock.

The protected space Louise and Thelma lost to Harlan is re-created in Louise's car. (*Thelma and Louise* as a revision of the boys-on-the-road genre has been much discussed, but little has been said about the heroines' unusual relationship to the car itself. They turn what is traditionally a male-gendered space into their own, in part through their rejection of traditionally female space.) As they drive, they find themselves alone in vast open spaces, and one way they pass time is by singing along with the car radio. They bounce, they shout, they use the songs to express defiant and dyadic pleasure. But they cannot contain the meanings of the songs. After Detective Slocum examines Louise's apartment, on the cut back to Louise and Thelma in the car, we hear them singing quite loudly to the Temptations' "The Way You Do the Things You Do." "The Way You Do the Things You Do" is a crossover hit that maximizes audience access; "everyone" knows it. As with the question of ordinariness, our ability to identify with their pleasure in this scene depends quite heavily on our relationships to this song, and much of the audience is likely to have one. Of course, those relationships will range from simple recognition (which is a pleasure in its own right) to genre or group fandom to highly individualized relationships (e.g., "our song," or

"That song was playing when ...."). Whatever the case, access to Louise and Thelma's bonding in this scene would be very different for someone who had never heard the song or any other example of its genre before.

The composed portions of the score also make use of country, blues, and rock. Entire portions of the score sound as if they could belong in any film with a synth-pop soundtrack; for instance, the main title rhythm is a rock drum machine standard:

Example 3
Thelma and Louise: Drum machine

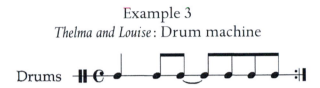

But other sections of the score are particularized by (synthesized) slide guitar and even banjo. The slide and banjo operate semiotically, both because the instruments themselves signify and because, as with any other instrument, the music played on them participates in musical signification processes as well. In this way, the score of *Thelma and Louise* provides ample support for Kalinak's argument that even pop scores use classical procedures and techniques.

Fairly early in the film, the percussion track of a composed section doubles in perceived speed, that is, it shifts from eighth-note to sixteenth-note patterns, when Louise decides to go Mexico and asks Thelma to go with her. (A sixteenth-note has half the time duration of an eighth-note; since it takes twice as many sixteenths to fill up the same time as eighths, this shift makes the perceived speed of the music double without an entire beat changing duration.) It changes specifically underneath her words "Everything's changed." The increased sense of speed signifies increased tension, increased action, increased danger, and/or increased speed. Later, mariachi trumpet figures moving in major thirds begin appearing on the soundtrack, implying a future in Mexico that we later learn is not to be.

As these examples show, classical Hollywood technique enforces certain meanings much more heavy-handedly than the pop songs usually do. Classical technique depends on semiotic production of meaning, that is, it depends on certain musical features, alone or in combination, bearing certain specific meanings: short, fast iterations equal tension, mariachi trumpets equal Mexico.

The sex scene between Thelma and J.D., however, offers an example of how classical technique can be combined with a preexisting song ("Kicking Stones" by Chris Whitley). On a cut from Jimmy and Louise to a close-up of J.D.'s glistening torso, a sixteenth-note pattern on keyboards and bass begins. As he begins to lower himself down onto Thelma, the slide guitar enters. As he begins to kiss her belly, a woman sings "ooh-ooh." A male vocalist is added; then, as J.D. pulls Thelma on top of him, there is a leap in the volume. While the musical language may not be the symphonic Romanticism of classical Hollywood, there is not a single cueing or mixing decision here that would surprise any Hollywood composer. (The sex scene between Sebastian and Annette in *Cruel Intentions* [1999], played out to "Color Blind" by Counting Crows, operates almost identically.)

Using songs classically in this way is becoming more and more common. By and large, however, songs work differently. Pop songs sometimes enter into meaning production through language, as in "I Don't Wanna Play House," but most often depend broadly on the identities of the musical genre's audience and on identification processes between the music and the perceiver that took place before the film. These modes of meaning production suggest a return to the first section of this chapter; pop scores operate through both agency and desire, however incompatible they may seem.

Reconciling (?) Desire and Agency

What makes all of these films stand out is not the mere fact that popular music is used on their soundtracks. (Some of the most "masculine" films of the 1980s—for example, *Above the Law* and *Boyz N the Hood*—use popular music as well.) Rather, reading scores as I did these—for the identification processes they condition— draws on the relationship between agency and desire. The films work against classical Hollywood's earlier dictates about femininity and female sexuality (to the complicated extent that they do) by mobilizing popular musics to tap emotions and associations that audiences connect with the musics before they ever enter the movie theater. Clearly, the practice of scoring female narrative agents with pop soundtracks makes possible a more diffused set of identifications for perceivers.

Desire and agency speak to each other in these films. They raise questions of meaning production, pleasure, uses, and social context and, therefore, intersect with the paradigms of feminist film criticism and of popular music studies in critical and interrogative ways. In other words, neither film theory nor popular music studies offers a narrative of reading/consumption/spectatorship that accounts for the specific identification processes popular music soundtracks entail. I want to address popular music studies and feminist film theory through these questions because each highlights the strengths of one paradigm and the weaknesses of the other. Since its formative moments, popular music studies has tended to emphasize the questions of uses and social context, while film theory focused on questions of meaning production and pleasure. But as the readings of the scores and their films

above demonstrate, social context is intimately imbedded in questions of meaning production—in popular music so intimately
that to privilege lived cultures over texts, or vice versa, severely
undermines the power of a theoretical approach to popular music
soundtracks.

As I pointed out earlier, feminist film theories have taken identification processes as their analytical point of entry. For example,
the identification processes encouraged by *Good Morning, Vietnam* and
Desert Hearts differ notably, depending heavily on sexual difference
for their productions of pleasure; traditional psychoanalytic readings of the films would put them at opposite ends of a spectrum.
Good Morning, Vietnam fetishizes the Vietnamese female body, presenting Vietnamese women as infinitely substitutable and desirable
in the sequence in which Robin Williams as Adrian Cronauer, the
deejay, rides all around the city mistaking every woman in a white
dress for the one he's looking for. *Desert Hearts* succeeds, at least
partly, in avoiding that fetishization by showing two women
loving each other, thus problematizing the masculine identification processes of much traditional film practice. Obviously, removing a heterosexual masculine look does not remove masculine
subjectivity from the circuits of desire in a film. But the kind of
familiar visual erotic pleasure produced by looking at a female
body through identification with a male character is interrupted
when the looking and desiring character is a female one.

As Sharon Willis argues in *High Contrast*, however, identification
processes engage perceivers in scenarios, not single positions.

An analysis equal to the complexity of the psychic operations
involved in identification has to acknowledge, first of all, that
identification is not a state, but a process, and that as such it is likely
to be mobile and intermittent rather than consistent. We will do
better to think of viewer identifications as scenarios rather than

as fixations. Hardly confined to identifications with characters, then, these scenarios may equally well fasten on situations, objects, and places, or the cinematic apparatus itself. (1997: 102)

But what is the place of music in such identification processes?

Some psychoanalytic theorists of music suggest that it takes us back to a prelinguistic moment, a time when we were surrounded by our mother's voice, swimming in a bath of affect. Feminist work on psychoanalysis, particularly in film theory, suggests that this is an impossible scenario, since already socialized adults cannot be mystically sent back to some preoedipal moment (Doane 1987; de Lauretis 1984; Modleski 1991). Kaja Silverman (1988) reformulates this problem by arguing that the sonorous envelope is a fantasy constructed retroactively by the subject. As with other kinds of identification processes, the fantasy of the sonorous envelope is a misrecognition, a Lacanian *méconnaissance*. David Schwarz's 1997 *Listening Subjects* engages Silverman's model on the terrain of specifically musical sounds; he suggests that certain composition and performance techniques draw listeners into different fantasies of regression. But what of film music, which perceivers hear less consciously than either Silverman's voices or Schwarz's musics?

A number of logics of film music listening have been identified, beginning with the earliest writings on "silent" film, about what film music does. (It is clear that there never was anything that could reasonably be called "silent" film. See King 1984; Marker 1997.) Among the arguments are that music seals over anxieties about discontinuous images, that it reinforces meaning, that it diffuses the unidirectionality of visual relations. These and other explanations abandon altogether any notion of film music in a continuum of musical experiences for listeners. In other words, I would quite forcefully add to this list the possibility that perceivers have prior relationships with music of the genres they hear in scores—country, blues, rock, etc. Moreover, they surely also have a relationship of long standing with the film music genre itself. Insofar as, within this genre, specific types of music have specific meanings, a perceiver may derive pleasure from an instance of film music because it evokes an accumulation of meanings from previous film experiences.

How meaning and pleasure come into being, however, only partly explains the relationship of perceiver to soundtrack. Soundtrack sales suggest that perceivers involve soundtracks in a variety of productions of meaning and pleasure after or without the "original" context of the film, using them in a range of contexts. I am arguing that this extrafilmic life is what makes them "tick": they depend on perceivers' memories of uses of the songs from many different contexts.

Because they engage perceivers in such different ways, pop scores require theories of both agency and identification. As I suggested in the first section of this chapter, feminist film theories and Marxist popular music studies each map out a continuous returning of what they repress. Psychoanalytic theories of culture repress the knowledge that unconscious processes are also historically determined, and that the boundary between an unconscious and a conscious is permeable. Marxist models repress the flip side of that coin: texts engage readers in unconscious processes as well as conscious ones, it is possible to know something about the structures and operations of those unconscious processes, and the boundary between unconscious and conscious processes is permeable.

Popular music soundtracks operate by crossing that boundary, evoking memories of emotions and subject positions, inviting perceivers to place themselves on their unconscious terrains. In order to address these webs of memory, affect, identifications, and the production of meanings, a theory that can account for the relationship between unconscious and conscious processes is necessary. The kinds of meanings perceivers produce in relation to *Dirty Dancing*, for instance, depend heavily on age and class, both generally and particularly in relation to the soundtrack. Perceivers of *Desert Hearts* cannot all understand Cay and Vivian's relationship similarly, because they cannot hear the music with the same histories.

Music works this way in film. It crosses over the boundaries between unconscious and conscious processes; it contradicts or shifts what seem like heavy-handed meanings in the visuals. (At least, it *can* do these things; in the next chapter, I will argue that it can also serve as a guarantor of meaning.) A Marxist psychoanalytic model of music perception and audiences can account for relationships among conscious and unconscious pleasures, among differences in consumption and reading practices, and among soundtracks as they address different audiences simultaneously.

As I will argue in the next chapter, not all films encourage the diversity of subject positions that these films do, but looking only at tightly controlled dominant texts can produce disturbingly monolithic theoretical models. The theory of music perception I proposed in this chapter attempts to explain both the similarities and the differences in the Tagg and Clarida study, to account for dominant ideologies as they are expressed in music and for soundtracks that are organized differently, and to leave room for perceivers who do not lose their histories at the theater door. Alongside these films with their dispersed identification processes, however, 1980s Hollywood also produced what we might call "hyperclassical" films such as the Star Wars and Indiana Jones series. These films returned to the tightest musical meaning system available just at the moment when mass culture seemed to be opening up to those it had historically excluded. It is to this phenomenon that I turn in the next chapter.

4

At the Twilight's Last Scoring

I am the street of your childhood,
I am the root of your ways.
I am the throbbing rhythm
in all that you long toward.
I am your mother's gray hands
and your father's worried mind,
and I am the light, wispy yarn
of your earliest dreams.

. . . I am the street of your childhood,
I am the root of your ways.
I gave you the watchful eyes,
by them shall you be known again,
If you meet someone with the same look,
You will know he is your friend.

—"Childhood's Street (Barndommens gade),"
Tove Ditlevsen (1942) (Translation mine)

S ince the late 1970s, one of the most important film score styles has been the heavy, Romantic symphonic score with thick instrumentation. The most important careers of the 1980s and 1990s, John Williams's and Danny Elfman's, were made almost exclusively on classical scores. Why has classical Hollywood scoring enjoyed such a resurgence? Is that resurgence organized around a particular ideological or subject position? If so, what position(s) and how?

In *Settling the Score,* Kathryn Kalinak argues that the classical film score as a formal structure has remained the dominant model since the 1930s. She argues that the classical Hollywood score is a series of procedures, and in this sense separates it from its musical idiom, late German symphonic Romanticism. She locates the particular defining features as the subservience of the score to the narrative and the principles Gorbman calls "inaudibility" and "invisibility," according to which the music must never make itself obvious, whether through technological or specifically musical materials.

Caryl Flinn, however, defines the classical film score as a discursive field embedded in Romantic ideology, and so finds for it a different relationship to contemporary Hollywood. She notes that the background quality of the classical score has fallen by the wayside, giving way to an industry both enabled by and hungry for new rock product. But even contemporary film music, she argues, conditions passage into "idealized states and pasts, be this through the rock music of *American Graffiti* or in John Williams's neoclassical theme for *Star Wars*" (1992: 152).

What Flinn argues for nostalgia, however, also describes an almost obsessive relationship between Hollywood and nationalism. While film studies have grappled with issues of nationalism in genre criticism of westerns and war movies and in studies of first-, second-, and third-world national cinemas, very few works have drawn on recent critiques of "nationalism" and the category of the nation-state. U.S. nationalism is a defining feature of Hollywood film history, as seen in a long line of movies from *Birth of a Nation* (1915) to *Mission to Mars* (2000). And that nationalism continues to be played out, in large part, through the scores.

But where is nationalism located in music? The relationship of music and the nation-state has a long and elaborate history. It includes the rise of national styles in Europe in the 1500s, the time of the rise of the nation-state formation. These styles are often identified with specific genres—irrespective of the "nationality" of the individual composer—such as the Italian *frottola* and *lauda*, the French chanson, the German lied and quodlibet, the Spanish *villancico,* and the English Service and anthem (Grout and Palisca 1988: 248–59). It also includes musical discourses of patriotism (national anthems), the development of overtly nationalist art music movements (e.g., the late-nineteenth-century Russian nationalist composers Balakirev, Borodin, Cui, Moussorgsky, and Rimsky-Korsakov, known as "the Russian five" or the "mighty handful"), and the collection and setting of folk songs as art music (Béla Bartók in Hungary, Gomidas Vartabed in Armenia).

Although the category of the nation has been present through-out histories of the aesthetic, it has always been something of an absent presence in conventional histories of western art music: while musical styles are named by it, it is never examined as a category. In Grout and Palisca's *History of Western Music* (1988), for instance, nationalism appears repeatedly throughout the text, but the authors seem unable to settle on what kind of relationship or relationships it can have to music:

> Musical Romanticism flourished especially in Germany, not only because the Romantic temper was congenial to German ways of thinking, but also because in that country national sentiment, being for a long time suppressed politically, had to find outlets in music and other forms of art. (p. 664)

> To some extent Chopin's polonaises may also be regarded a
> national manifestation ... some of [them] blaze anew with the
> knightly and heroic spirit of his native land. (p. 687)

> Verdi, as we saw, became a symbol for national unity, but this was
> for reasons other than the character of his operas. (p. 771)

> [Verdi] believed wholeheartedly that each nation should cultivate
> the kind of music that was native to it. (p. 736)

The authors stumble over a series of possibilities (none of which
they engage as the stuff of serious music history). Can nationalism be a formal feature of music, as the "Russian five" contended,
and if so, can one nationalism be distinguished from another? Can
it reside in the spirit of a land that can blaze in a polonaise, and if
so, does it reside in the melody, or the performance, or the
rhythm, or the instrumentation, or harmonic treatments, or
some other features? Can it be a thematic feature whereby native
music is cultivated into an art form (Bartók and Gomidas)? Or
does it reside entirely in realms outside the music qua music, as
Grout and Palisca suggest about Verdi (and as Stravinsky and
Adorno, as quoted in chapter 1, said of all meaning in music)?

This confusion over if and how nationalism might operate
musically—and over the social or political functions or effects of
musical nationalism—has everything to do with the ongoing
debates about meaning in music on the one hand, and about the
discourses of nationalism on the other. The musical production
of U.S. nationalism in contemporary film intertwines inseparably
with the categories of race, gender, and sexuality. In the following section, I discuss three very different action-adventure films
with three very different scores, all of which track identifications
with a particular U.S. national subject.

The Hunt for Lethal Red Weapons
in the Temple of October Doom 2

Different versions of U.S. American nationalism underpin *Lethal Weapon 2, The Hunt for Red October,* and *Indiana Jones and the Temple of Doom.* Each organizes what it means to be American, as they uniformly call it, in terms of race and gender, but not identically. *The Hunt for Red October* was released in 1990 to great response on the part of spy-thriller fans. Tom Clancy's book made what a popular video guide book called an "edge-of-your-seat winner" (Martin and Porter 1992: 897) about a Lithuanian sub captain who defects with a new high-tech Soviet stealth sub and its crew. The audio track seems perfect for a spy film; it is overwhelmingly sneaky, in two senses. First, it *sounds* like a spy film, in that much of the music is short repeated chromatic figures (see example 4 below). Second, the music constantly edges in under the omnipresent ambient noise of the subs, beginning as a barely audible hum that lasts for long seconds before the musical cue seems to come from nowhere. This technique, called "sneaking," is central to classical Hollywood practice; it protects the score from being noticed. Because it uses extremely heavy ambient noise, because it blurs the distinction between sound and music, and because much of its music is very small repetitive figures, the overall sound of *Red October* is very thick and organized by an emphasis on sound over music.

The only melodic music in the film is the anthem of the Soviet Union, which appears again and again. It is sung through the opening titles, in an odd kind of pseudo–Soviet Army Chorus style that includes female voices and symphonic orchestration. When Ramius (Sean Connery), who importantly is Lithuanian rather than Russian, informs his crew that their mission is to sneak into U.S. waters, they break out singing. In fact, it is precisely this moment of singing that gives them away to the U.S. sub—

Example 4
The Hunt for Red October: Submarine ostinato

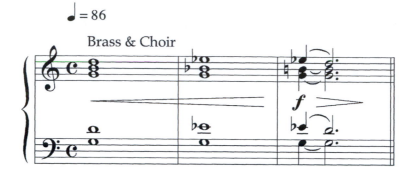

the virtuoso black sonar man, Jonesy, hears the singing. The anthem is heard again in the Soviet admiral's office, on the radio, as he gets the news that Ramius is defecting, and four or five times more over the course of the film. In this way, music and Soviet nationalism become inseparable.

Moreover, the film's dialogue keeps returning to music in strange ways. When Jonesy is introduced teaching a young white seaman sonar technique, he tricks the seaman, and then tells him, "So, like Beethoven on the computer, you have labored to produce . . . a biologic." The camera pans 360 degrees around the small sonar room, passing across a poster of Beethoven. A short while later, an officer teases him, telling a story of how Jonesy once projected music out into the water to listen to it, and had a whole fleet listening to Paganini. Jonesy repeatedly corrects him, saying the music was Pavarotti, not Paganini; the former is a tenor, the latter a composer, he insists. The film distinguishes him as a genius with sonar technology, but neither as "one of the guys" nor as a leader among them. (In fact, the intersections of race, class, and sexuality become particularly complicated in a black techie classical music lover. The establisment of Jonesy's character in these early scenes is a significant example of how frequently issues of race surface in films through music, as they do in *Desert Hearts* in the final sequence when the soundtrack introduces Ella Fitzgerald singing "I Wished on the Moon.")

Moreover, rock 'n' roll has a particular status in the film's world. When Ramius tells the crew that they are headed for American waters, he says, "We will pass through the American patrols, pass their sonar nets, and lay off their largest city and listen to their rock 'n' roll while we conduct missile drills." When the captain of the Dallas wants to express how careless the Red October is being, he says, "They're moving at close to thirty knots; at that speed, they could run over my daughter's stereo and not hear it."

So. Rock 'n' roll is U.S. noise. Russians sing. And both narratively and musically, it is obvious who the real Americans really are. The first musical cue belongs to Ramius, during the sequence in which he kills the political commissar of the mission. The music invites identification at the moment of his radical separation from the USSR (see example 5 below). While the music is almost identical to the ostinato for the submarines in example 4, the difference here is that the music expresses Ramius's subjective state.

Example 5
The Hunt for Red October:
Ramius kills the political commissar

Strings and choir

The next cue is organized around Jack Ryan (Alec Baldwin), who a variety of filmic devices have made clear is the hero from the outset of the film. (For example, the entire opening sequence of the film is devoted to Ryan in his home with his wife and child, Ryan afraid of flying and on a transatlantic flight, and point-of-view shooting of his arrival by limousine at the Pentagon.) On one occasion later in the film, during a joint chiefs of staff meeting to determine what to do about the Red October, the music (see example 6) enters on a cut to Ryan thinking, and exits on the president's national security advisor saying, "You wish to add something to our discussion, Dr. Ryan?" This is the moment at which Ryan's identification with Ramius takes over both Ryan and the film, and the music draws them together in opposition to the quite different musicality the film creates for Russianness.

To be vulgar, then: Americans are white and men. Jonesy comes close to earning American status, but he fails on several counts. First, his music listening practices separate him out from the crew as weird, and quite possibly gay. As Philip Brett (1994) argues, musicality has an intimate ideological and discursive connection with male homosexuality. Not only do musicality and homosexuality both circulate as deviances, but they are also, to some extent, stand-ins for each other. While gay men (pre-Stonewall) used phrases such as "Does he play in the orchestra?" as markers of gay identity, musicality signifies feminization, "queerness," homosexuality in everyday boy locker-room parlance. According to Brett's argument, Jonesy's musicality implies at least the possibility of homosexuality. Second, the film's score never supports his bid for symbolic citizenship—of the roughly thirty musical cues throughout the film, not one accompanies Jonesy directly. The score's message is: pumped-up patriotic anthem singing is old-fashioned, and real American nationalism opens its very white arms to all the Ramiuses who are smart enough and man enough to deserve the embrace.

Example 6
The Hunt for Red October:
Ryan meets the national security advisor

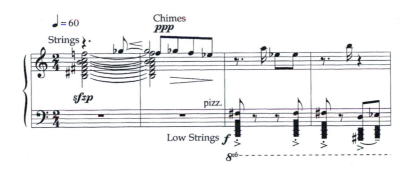

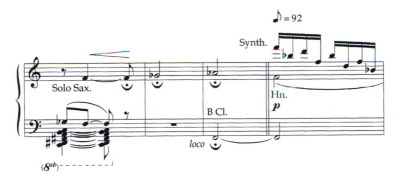

Lethal Weapon 2 tells a slightly different story about race, nationalism, and masculinity. The South African consulate in Los Angeles is a front for all kinds of illegal activities; officers Riggs (Mel Gibson) and Murtaugh (Danny Glover) must uncover the scheme and get the bad guys. The Eric Clapton cool jazz-rock sax-guitar score suggests a musical discourse that crosses racial lines. Unlike classical scores organized around one or more leitmotivs, but similar to the case of *The Hunt for Red October*, this score uses small varying figures of four notes to signify danger/suspense, as I discuss further below, and the seemingly unraced style of fusion—a combination of jazz and rock—for Riggs and Murtaugh. But over the course of the film—and, actually, over the course of the three films—it becomes clear that the Eric Clapton and David Sanborn licks are really Riggs's and not Murtaugh's. They enter with Riggs, they follow him around, they express what his character is experiencing, and so on. Even in the opening sequence, the music really belongs to Riggs. During the long chase sequence, there is no music until it enters on the cut to Gibson crawling out through the windshield of Murtaugh's wife's bashed-up car. As in *Red October*, the musical cues have the earmarks (and consequences) of a particular point-of-view, and it is Riggs's.

Moreover, fusion signifies race, in a rather confused field. It is generally understood by aficionados to have begun in New York in 1969 with Miles Davis's *In a Silent Way* and *Bitches Brew* (on which virtually every future fusion star played). Since then, it has been "whited" in a series of ways. First, many of its major players have been white: Josef Zawinul, John McLaughlin, Al DiMeola, and others.[1] Second, it is defined in part by its considerable roots in rock 'n' roll, which by that time was quite monolithically white in both production and consumption. Finally, it is discursively produced in jazz history as inauthentic and mercenary; Len Lyons, in a jazz listener's guide, says:

Fusion has been both lucrative and controversial in its short life-time. According to the music's many critics, its popularity and profits far exceed its aesthetic values, durability, or contribution to jazz's developments. . . . the lure of fame and fortune has lured some promising serious musicians into wasting their talents in pursuing financial goals. (1980: 333)

In jazz tradition, these musical judgments are very often made with respect to white jazz musicians. So, in many ways, fusion signifies as a white jazz genre. On the other hand, it signifies as a *jazz* genre, not as a rock genre. Fusion holds a small place as a failed experiment in jazz history, but it is absent altogether from most rock histories. To the extent that it sounds "jazzy," then, and to the extent that "jazz" still signifies as "black" music, fusion may well signify blackness or, closely enough, hipness, to an audience unfamiliar with jazz history and discourse.

Verbally, *Lethal Weapon 2* is oddly preoccupied with nationalism. Nationality defines the bad guys here; once the film introduces the South African consul, it isn't very surprising that he is running drugs, laundering money, and smuggling krugerrands. And since he and his fellow countrymen have diplomatic immunity, the only way to "get them" is to blow them sky high, thus earning this sequel the right to bear the *Lethal Weapon* brand.

Beyond this, there are two very telling moments where the film defines for us who gets to be American. When Riggs needs a cover to sneak into the consul's office, Leo (Joe Pesci) and Murtaugh create a diversion by having Murtaugh apply for a visa to emigrate to South Africa. The official, of course, tries to dissuade Murtaugh, who gives a rousing speech about going to South Africa to help his brothers in their struggle for freedom. If one is black, in other words, one's allegiances cross national boundaries. Simultaneously, Riggs gets caught breaking into the consul's office and identifies himself as an American. He says: "I'll make a deal with you, Arjun, or Aryan, or whatever the fuck your name is. You get the fuck out of my country, and I won't blow your head off." (The music throughout this scene has been marimba octaves, until Riggs attacks; his actions are accompanied by fusion guitar.) For Riggs to identify along racial lines, he would be required to side with the bad guys. But he can't; he's the hero. And anyway, why should he? He's American.

In all the ways that the music defines Riggs as (1) a hero, (2) the hero of the movie, and (3) the hero of the country, Murtaugh is excluded from those definitions. He can't be American as the film defines it because he's black. Beyond that, he can't, as Danny Glover has noted in interviews, be romantic, which often defines a hero. And the music isn't his, and the narrative isn't his. And he has commitments beyond the realm of justice—a family. In the opening chase scene, Murtaugh worries about destroying his wife's station wagon, but his concern is dismissed by Riggs and ridiculed in the station house. That sequence guarantees that we know right from the start who the real man is, and he isn't the one with the family; at least since *Rebel Without a Cause*, Hollywood has made sure perceivers know what to think about men who worry about what their wives will say. (In terms of the debates about family values in the 1992 presidential campaign, it is telling that *Murphy Brown* was a target of criticism while the *Lethal Weapon* movies weren't.) So, as in *The Hunt for Red October*, to the extent that men of color are included in the film, they are excluded from symbolic citizenship.

The connection to *Rebel Without a Cause* raises some interesting questions about the role of masculine sexuality in *Lethal Weapon 2*. Just as Jonesy marks the threat of homosexuality in *The Hunt for Red October*, so too does Leo mark that same threat in this film. And like Jonesy, Leo is marked as gay not directly, but indirectly by stereotypes of gay masculinity. The film shows his distance from Hollywood heterosexual masculinity in his obsession about cleanliness and order, in his constantly fluttering hands, in his continuous talking, and in his affected speech. But the film goes even further in defining the terms of its symbolic citizenship. After Riggs threatens to blow the consul's head off, he continues, "If you stay around, I'm gonna fuck your ass." The worst punishment Riggs can threaten, it seems, is that he will anally penetrate the consul. The equivalence—the exchangeability—established is between illicitly crossing national boundaries and crossing illicit sexual ones.[2]

Unlike *Red October*, then, *Lethal Weapon 2* is not generous with its symbolic citizenship. Narratively, the film belongs to Riggs, who is the only cast member to occupy the "American" position, in spite of Mel Gibson's Australian accent. Musically, too, the film is his. During the long sequence that shows cops being killed, Riggs is in his beach trailer making love to the consular secretary. Small danger figures accompany the various deaths, while Riggs and the girl get source music—an oldies radio station. At first hearing, it may seem that the danger figures signify the South African villains, as a kind of stylistic leitmotiv similar to Riggs's fusion.

But I want to suggest that this oversimplifies the way the music signifies. The use of source music for Riggs's sex parallels the use of source music in other scenes in the movie(s): the themes to the Looney Tunes and the Three Stooges and early sixties rock 'n' roll all seem to express his subjectivity by accompanying major subjective moments, such as his contemplation of suicide, or sex with a new lover. The danger figures for the deaths of the cops, who noticeably and multiculturally include blacks and women, are scored for strings and marimbas, an instrument with a very distinctive sound. Various marimba patterns appear throughout, associated with the South African consul and his gang. But Riggs's fusion sound also has marimbas—usually accompanying guitar and sax. That orchestration gives the film an overall sound; without it, the difference between the strings and the guitar-sax combo could be jarring. Moreover, the use of the marimbas for both Riggs and the South Africans creates an eerie sense of a threat from within (perhaps related to the diplomatic immunity of the consular staff).

The presence of the marimbas suggests that the deaths of the cops have some direct relationship to Riggs, that they are his issue and his responsibility to avenge. This distribution of musics— fusion for Riggs, strings and marimbas figures for danger, and source music for Riggs's "weak" moments—performs an overwhelming array of ideological work. It places Riggs firmly within the discourses of both hegemonic masculinity and Hollywood herodom, wherein he seems sensitive and loving, while his "self"—marked by his "own" music—is entirely located in action rather than emotion. It also places him within the discourse of American patriotism, because his self is defined in terms of his commitment to justice.

Indiana Jones and the Temple of Doom is the only one of these three films not *overtly* about Americanism in some way. Moving around Asia as if it were the size of New Jersey, Indy crashes a plane in China, sleds down the Himalayas in a life raft, and lands in an Indian jungle, in a sequence held together (to the extent that it *is* held together) by continuous music. Thereafter, the film revolves around barbarians in India who have revived a cult of human sacrifice. A predictable score would have included a lot of what Jerry Goldsmith called Hollywood ethnic-oriental music: fourths and gongs in China, snake charmer harmonic minors in India. After all, it seems reasonable to expect the John Williams classical style to do the classical thing where ethnicity is concerned. But it doesn't.

Example 7
Indiana Jones and the Temple of Doom:
Epic sound

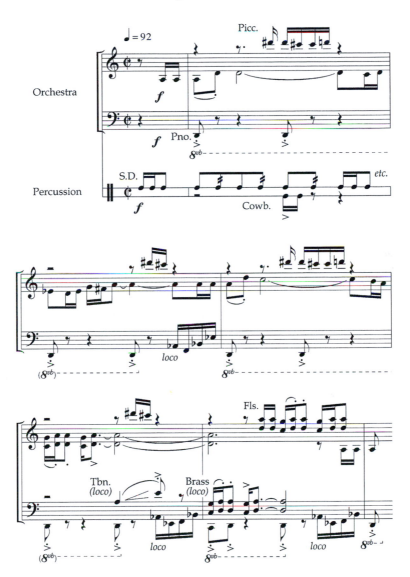

There is very little ethnic scoring at all in the film, and most of what there is is source music. For instance, during the snakes-and-monkey-brains banquet in Pangkot Palace, there is music for the dancing girls to dance to. And during the heathen Kali rituals of sacrifice, there is chanting, focused on words without melody to speak of. But the dramatic scoring almost never has an "ethnic" sound, and when it does, it only lasts for a few phrases. In large part, the film is a *Ben-Hur* epic soundalike, which suggests that there is a style of music we might call spectacle or epic in its own right (see example 7).[3] However this music is named, it has room for neither subjectivity nor geography; it only bothers to represent the film's broad comic action. The two-dimensional ethnic villains don't get a chance, a point on which the narrative and the score are in wholehearted agreement. And Willy, whose rendition of "Anything Goes" in Chinese opens the film, does not get another musical moment to herself. So, Indiana Jones, even more blatantly than Riggs and Ryan, earns the right to herodom and citizenship by virtue of gender and color.

In fact, it is interesting to note the oedipal trajectory of this film. As Sobchack (1986) and Clough (1992) have argued, the 1980s produced a spate of films in which children became their parents' parents. From *Close Encounters of the Third Kind* to the first *Back to the Future*, children do what their parents cannot, go where their parents cannot, and repair what their parents broke. Here, this fantasy of reversal is twisted; Indy, the father, saves Short Round and hundreds of enslaved Indian village children. But Short Round also saves Indy. Willy, who is about to be sacrificed to Kali-ma, begs and pleads with a drugged Indy, crying and screaming for her life. But only Short Round can break him out of his drug-induced trance—by yelling "Indy, I love you, you're my best friend, Indy"—and this only after escaping from a flock of child laborers in an action sequence that Indiana alone could match.

Musically, the extended sequence mainly uses source chanting, which at times becomes source scoring, as the crowds begin to chant/sing in four-part harmony with the sudden addition of women's voices. But at two moments, when Short Round is escaping from his shackles and when he approaches Indy, the full-blown symphonic dramatic scoring pulls no punches. Trumpets and french horns, supported by strings and timpani, carry the epic melody that accompanies Short Round's escape. The timpani become the drums beating a rhythm for the chanters, who have returned to their original genders. But when Shorty lands in front of Indy—crying out "Wake up, Dr. Jones, wake up!"—the horns return, then thin out by reducing in numbers. Then they audiomorph into high, keening violins that begin a short tremolo passage (a classical danger and suspense device), returning to a solo trumpet in time for Shorty's curative cry.

By juxtaposing the chanting to symphonic scoring, the score clearly divides "us" and "them." The pagan chanting hordes will allow their evil leader to tear out someone's heart as part of a ritual of sacrifice, while good Americans reserve their hearts for classical symphonic technique and young boys crying out "I love you."

Identification as Assimilation

Musically, these films reside resolutely within the classical Hollywood tradition, both in Kalinak's procedural sense and Flinn's nostalgic sense. The films I discussed in chapter 3 tend to proliferate possibilities of identification, often in part by giving two female characters comparable (though never equal) technical and narrative attention. I am suggesting here that *Lethal Weapon 2*, *The Hunt for Red October*, and *Indiana Jones and the Temple of Doom* appear to do the same with their casts, but the potential for alternative identification choices posed by the competing characters (Murtaugh, Leo, Jonesy, and Short Round) is ultimately neutralized. This is accomplished through all the ways film theory has articulated: through narrative, editing, and camera techniques. The ability for perceivers to shift positions within the fantasy scenarios offered by these films is carefully limited.

But music, too, is entirely imbricated in the relationship of characters to filmic positions of power. In the previous chapter I worked from films that do not simply follow classical Hollywood scoring procedures, arguing that the use of popular songs in scores invites perceivers to bring their own "music histories" into play with the film. Music editing procedures for popular songs also generally take different approaches than for classical scores, with less care taken to parallel visual continuity editing.

For example, to return to *Thelma and Louise* for a moment, in the sequence with "House of Hope," the song is mixed (i.e., the volume is changed) according to classical procedures for dramatic scoring, but the editing is not in the same tradition. As a broad generality, classical cues are relatively short, whereas "House of Hope" lasts for about three full minutes, from when Louise and Thelma pull out of the driveway until just before they pull into the parking lot of the bar. It is anything but "inaudible"; its entrance is not "sneaked"; it exits in a simple fade—the volume gets lower and lower until the music disappears. In this sequence, it would be hard work not to notice "House of Hope." What emerges in part through the mixing and more strongly through the editing is an extended moment of music that commands a relatively high degree of attention, and that is likely to be perceived as a quotation.

This particular textual profile, created by the postproduction technical decisions of editing and mixing, makes a wide field of identifications possible. In extreme contrast, the scoring of the short underwater sequences of the subs in *The Hunt for Red October* leaves relatively little room for mobile identification processes. They signify strongly within classical Hollywood tradition: the first ostinato quoted above, for example, clearly marks something in the realm of suspense or danger, predominantly because of its tight range (a perfect fourth), size (three chords), and chromaticism. But as a performed piece of music, its meaning becomes even clearer. There are still dozens of musical and technical features to consider. The orchestration is classical Hollywood symphonic, predominantly strings; the phrasing is legato; there is little echo; all the recording and mixing features suggest acoustic performance. This tiny figure is purebred classical Hollywood.

By this I do not mean to suggest that the procedures of classical Hollywood scoring and the Romantic symphonic idiom most closely associated with them regulate signification in some complete way. No semiotic system can completely control or guarantee the production of a particular meaning. Rather, the question of the difference between compiled and composed scores centers on how their different relationships to intertextuality and textual competences condition identification processes.

The music in *The Hunt for Red October* refers to Hollywood film music, with the exception of the Soviet anthem, which is used, much like Goldsmith's fourths and gongs, for identification in the sense discussed in chapter 2. It signifies nationality and geography without an unwieldy concern for ethnomusicological accuracy. (For example, the military thematics of the film and the invocation of the Soviet Army Chorus could have precluded the possibility of women's voices, as the choruses themselves did.) I argued empirically in chapter 1 that broad audiences are competent in Hollywood film music; that position is further supported by the music's ubiquity in both film and television. (One would have to work hard *not* to acquire competence in it; for example, the theme for *Jaws* that I discussed in chapter 2 developed a life of its own, becoming *the* sound of ironic danger. Such uses—quotations—both reinforce and undercut the semiotic system of classical Hollywood film music.) Film scores composed in that tradition, then, rely on a signification system designed for precisely the same uses to which the scores themselves will put it, and their perceivers only need competence in that one system.

Thelma and Louise's score, however, requires multiple competences: in Hollywood film music, in country and western, in blues, and in rock. Some of these musics are subcultural practices that are mainly consumed by perceivers with particular competences, acquired inside one or more particular communities. Moreover, competences acquired in the same musics in different communities may lead to very different kinds of identifications. For instance, the associations of country and western listeners who grew up in Fort Worth, Texas, might make *Desert Hearts* a disorienting experience, while the associations of country and western listeners who began listening to it in gay bars in New York City might make the score seem perfectly natural or strange for women.

The *Lethal Weapon* films problematize this distinction in important ways. The music in *Lethal Weapon 2* is not really fusion in the sense that it would not stand up to listening on its own as an example of the genre. One of fusion's most particular features is a virtuoso instrumental technique that would be inappropriate (because distracting) in a classical Hollywood score like this one. On the other hand, the music is unmistakably fusion in its instrumental, melodic, and textural procedures. Arguably, this score invites identifications as a classical Hollywood score, because the music signifies "urban," "hip," and "interracial," rather than opening particularly onto specific perceivers' histories. *Perceivers* is the word I have chosen to designate the theoretical placeholder for audience members; it cannot be reduced to either textuality or an extratextual "real." While perceivers, as theoretical constructs, can never be the same as "real" audience members, they mark an important distinction from previous theoretical positions both because they are decidedly multiple and because they have ears.

Perceivers come with social histories—they bring gender, race, class, sexuality, and many other axes of identity to the foreground. Unlike the spectator of psychoanalytic film theory, they engage films, complete with visual, verbal, sound, and musical tracks, in a flow of conscious and unconscious operations. And their unconsciouses are not those of traditional psychoanalysis, organized around sexual difference conceived from the perspective of the penis-cum-phallus. Their unconsciouses are, rather, organized by the particular differences that strain the match between their subjectivities and the subject positions offered by dominant modes of textuality and narrativity. Perceivers—these theoretical entities produced in the writing of a hearing film critical practice—engage films in identification processes that reproduce, on a microcosmic level, their everyday processes of assimilation.

But if traditional psychoanalysis does not describe perceivers' unconsciouses, who or what does? The epigraph of this chapter is an excerpt of a poem by Tove Ditlevsen (1918–1976), a Danish woman poet and novelist whose work centers on the subjective experiences of working-class girls and women.[4] "Childhood's Street" ("Barndommens Gade") describes a process of subjectivity formation not quite the same as the one described by psychoanalysis, but with many similar principles. Subjectivity is formed in childhood—"I am the street of your childhood / I am the root of your ways"—as a drive to fulfill desire—"I am your throbbing rhythm / in everything you may desire." Parents play a significant role in its formulation; aside from the "I" and the "you," "your mother's gray hands" and "your father's worried mind" are the only phrases in which specific people appear.

The poem also makes clear that those formative experiences are neither simply painful nor simply comforting—

> I hit you once to the ground
> to make your heart hard,
> but I gently pulled you up again
> and dried the tears away

—and that identity as an experience of similarity (not sameness) is grounded in similar experiences—"If you meet someone with the same look / You will know he is your friend." In this sense, the poem roots its operation in the principles of assimilation. It suggests that people with similar experiences recognize each other and that these processes are both conscious—about knowing and knowledge—and unconscious—about modes of being and hardened hearts.

The "I" that governs the development of the poem's addressee marks the significant difference between psychoanalysis and the model of the poem. Psychoanalysis posits a subjectivity formed primarily in relation to heterosexual parents living together within a particular ideological formation of domesticity (Gelpi 1992), or at least in relation to the figures of those parents as they circulate generally in culture (television, schools, church, and so on). It therefore posits sexual difference as the inaugural difference. "Childhood's Street," however, posits a subjectivity formed in relation to a broad social realm, suggesting quite strongly that surviving difficult early experiences draws a common bond, differentiating subjects not primarily as men or not, but rather as watchful or not.

Perhaps most importantly, however, it suggests that watchful subjects recognize each other, but are not recognized generally by others. They appear, in other words, or perhaps behave *as if* they were not watchful. This is the governing principle of assimilation—that subjects behave *as if* they were not different from the idealized dominant subjectivity that organizes most of culture. And that behavior is not simply reducible to role-playing. As the poem suggests, subjectivities tune themselves to the roles they are asked—and choose—to play. In Althusserian terms, the act of answering a hail is not reducible to a function of either agency or desire.

Which bring us back to music more generally. Music has a particular relationship to processes of assimilation. As many have argued, music acts as a lubricant to identification processes, smoothing the transition into (often barely plausible) fictional worlds by washing perceivers in a "bath or gel of affect" (Gorbman 1987: 5). But this model only begins to describe the relations between perceivers and music, and it does not describe the relations between perceivers and popular songs.

More to the point, music facilitates perceivers in assimilating into one of the available subject positions of the film. In the case of films, like those in chapter 3, that do not limit those positions to the rigid classical one, the music proliferates possibilities by opening perception onto perceivers' own (socially conditioned) histories. In the case of more classical films, like *Indiana Jones and the Temple of Doom*, the score limits possibilities by narrowing access to perceivers' histories and focusing instead on their competence in assimilation.

To return to *Lethal Weapon 2*, then, it becomes clear that the identification processes likely to be engaged in by gay and black male perceivers will be significantly different, both because gay and black identities operate differently from each other and because the categories of race and sexuality operate differently within the film. Murtaugh provides an eminently accessible path of assimilation; through an initial identification with him, a perceiver can be eased into a white male subject position, in part because of Murtaugh's proximity to Riggs and in part because the score directs that kind of passage. In the opening sequence discussed previously, the scenario is wide open to identification with either Riggs or Murtaugh, but once the score enters as Riggs climbs out the window, the available positions narrow down. Assimilation can operate in this way, by metonymy. But the processes available through Leo are quite different. By making him a clown and stereotypically gay, the film makes three paths most likely: refusal to engage with the film on the grounds that it is insulting, a camp identification with Leo, and identification with the homophobic position—organized by Riggs's and Murtaugh's annoyance—that finds him funny.[5] Assimilation can also operate in this way, by making disavowal attractive.

Both sets of possibilities depend, however, on the score's resolute production of a privileged subject position. Where the score is less narrowly committed to one position, more mobile processes of identification are possible. Even in *Dirty Dancing*, the organization of the score around Baby and Johnny's dancing facilitates movement between a working-class male white ethnic subject position and a middle-class white Jewish female one. As *Thelma and Louise* does for Thelma, *Dirty Dancing* speaks from Johnny's perspective with increasing strength over the course of the film; as his subjective experiences accumulate screen time, the possibility of seeing the world of Kellerman's Catskills resort from a working-class subject position becomes increasingly available. But that play of availability would be impossible if Johnny were scored the way Murtaugh is.

The final sequence of *Dirty Dancing*, however, makes clear another trajectory of assimilating identifications: they are never completely successful, and therefore always up for grabs. There is no reason for a white middle-class perceiver to find the joy and exuberance of the final sequence uncomfortable. Johnny—he of the beautiful and knowledgeable body—singles Baby out for her outstanding ability to practice good middle-class values—sticking to one's principles, honesty, trustworthiness, and so on. And the music he brings has, of course, a hypnotic effect on everyone in the room, so that the guests at Kellerman's forget their middle-class inhibitions, not only by beginning to dance, but even by dancing with some of the entertainment staff. The film makes it clear that the music made them do it, and a happy, nonclassed fantasy ending is enjoyed by all.

Or is it? For perceivers of any class who believe in the American dream, the ending of *Dirty Dancing* can seem uncomplicated and right. But for those who have difficulty fantasizing a happily-ever-after for Baby and Johnny, the film's ending is more complicated, and that difficulty settles preferentially onto Ditlevsen's watchful subjects. The problem is in the nature of any moment of narrative closure; what McClary argues for closure in tonal procedures—the cadence—is also true of closure in film narrative:

> A significant factor that contributes to the violence of tonal procedures is that the actual reward—the cadence—can never be commensurate with the anticipation generated or the effort expended in achieving it. The cadence is, in fact, the most banal, most conventionalized cliché available within any given musical style. (1991: 127)

In this sense, not even the score can finally seal the arbitrariness of closure, because its own closure is equally arbitrary. The film is most at risk of losing perceivers engaged in assimilating identification processes at this moment, because the banality of closure makes them likely to call a halt to the process altogether and step outside again. But the cadence will in some way disappoint even perceivers who are comfortably interpellated by the film, and it is in this sense that assimilation is never successful or complete, but always a continuous process.

The microcosmic process of assimilating identification that I have described here depends on and participates in the macroscopic level production of U.S. nationality by many, many layers of accumulated processes of assimilation. As many film and social historians have argued, film was an important part of immigrants' complex and ambivalent assimilation processes in the United States in the early part of the twentieth century. I have argued, much more broadly, that assimilation is a necessary ongoing function for the constitution of the United States as a nation; that it operates in movie theaters (and many other cultural venues); and that film scores regularly perform its work. In the next chapter, I will turn again to scores that work according to a different logic, a logic of affiliation that does not track identifications quite so rigidly.

5

Opening Scores

If action-adventure films offer assimilating identifications, what does this tell us about soundtracks like *Dangerous Liaisons* or *Thelma and Louise*? I suggest, in this final chapter, that there is another kind of identification, and one that is central to many soundtracks of contemporary Hollywood films—the affiliating identification. When a soundtrack does not narrow possibilities toward a single position, as in the assimilating identifications of the last chapter, the processes it offers are looser, grouping together or affiliating characters or positions in a scenario with which perceivers can identify.

Since the late 1980s and early 1990s, film theory has pulled further and further away from psychoanalytic paradigms. The 1990 double issue of *Camera Obscura* entitled "The Spectatrix" may serve as a watershed moment. In it, the editors asked sixty feminist film scholars to answer four questions on the idea of (the) female spectator(s). Each question was intended to elicit both intellectual history and a sense of future directions for feminist film and television studies, particularly in relation to psychoanalytic notions of spectatorship. The second question addresses this concern most directly:

2. The very term "female spectator" has been subject to some dispute insofar as it seems to suggest a monolithic position

ascribed to the woman. In your opinion, is the term most productive as a reference to empirical spectators (individual
women who enter the movie theater), as the hypothetical
point of address of the film as a discourse or as a form of mediation between these two concepts? Or as something else
entirely? (Bergstrom and Doane 1990)

At that moment, feminist film theory was facing what might be
called the incommensurability of the psychic and the social. The
amazing theoretical developments of the late 1970s and the 1980s
showed how central identification processes are to the con-
frontations between subjects and texts. The subsequent call to
consider differences other than an inaugural sexual difference led
to interest in theories of subcultures and ethnographic methodologies that gave neither ontological nor epistemological priority
to sex, gender, and sexuality.

But those theories and methodologies came with fairly steep
price tags. Ellen Seiter, herself an ethnographer, worried that

> there is an overwhelming urge to reduce the "subjects" to essen-
> tialist categories of gender, class and race based on the briefest
> acquaintance and questioning, to lapse into a "happy positivism." It
> is also a struggle not to treat the language of the interviewed "sub-
> ject" as transparent. More importantly, the relations of authority
> and control between the interviewer and "subject" involved in this
> kind of work are seriously unsettling. . . . (1990: 285–86)

In their introduction to the issue, Janet Bergstrom and Mary Ann
Doane address an even larger concern with ethnographic
approaches. They point out that ethnography gives the researcher
access to "the conscious observations people make about the

media, observations which the ethnographer may not take at face value, but which are not subjected to a detailed scrutiny in view of the psychical strategies of disavowal, denegation and repression" (1990: 12). As Annette Kuhn and several other theorists warn, audience research threatens to cast aside the unconscious as an entry point for analysis.

Arguably, however, that is exactly what happened. Psychoanalytic feminist film theories were subjected to a much-needed critique, and concerns for unconscious processes were ultimately sidelined by the main flow of theorizing in the 1990s. But without an account of the mutual imbrication of identifications and identities, no compelling account of film perception can be given. Throughout this book, I have been suggesting that one of Hollywood film music's central functions is to condition, or track, paths of identification. I have argued that the scores of films like *Desert Hearts* and *Bagdad Cafe* open identifications to perceivers' various histories, while more classical scores, like the action-adventure films discussed in chapter 4, narrowly track identifications toward a single path. The indeterminacy of the multiple positions offered by *Bagdad Cafe*, for example, requires an account of identifications in motion, identifications that are forged in some very elaborate combinations of processes.

In the remainder of this chapter, I will consider two pairs of films: *Dangerous Minds* and *The Substitute*; and *Mississippi Masala* and *Corrina, Corrina*. Each pair makes available the opportunity to examine complicated musical offers of identifications—both between characters in the films and between the films and their perceivers—that, if they are to work at all, have to cross boundaries of race, class, education, age, and gender. Like the films in chapter 3, these films depend on their scores to offer something other than an assimilating identification.

Opposites Rap

At the surface, *Dangerous Minds* and *The Substitute* could seem like twin films. Each is set in a high school, each focuses on a single white teacher, and each deals with "difficult," "challenging" underclass nonwhite students. Each even has a bad guy principal who happens to be African-American. In fact, the cover to the video of *The Substitute* prominently features the following quotation from Sandi Davis of the *Daily Oklahoman*: "'Dangerous Minds' Meets Steven Seagal."

Moreover, each film had a heavily marketed soundtrack album featuring important hip-hop artists. *The Substitute*'s album includes cuts by Mack 10 featuring Ice Cube, Ras Kass, Kid Frost, Intense Method, Lil 1/2 Dead, Afro-Rican, Organized Konfusion, Master P, and Tru. Similarly, *Dangerous Minds*' audiences heard Coolio featuring L.V., Aaron Hall, Big Mike, Rappin' 4-Tay, Mr. Dalvin & Static, Tre Black, 24-K, Immature, DeVante, and Sista featuring Craig Mack.

But there the comparison ends. *Dangerous Minds* is a charming, recognizable, liberal education fantasy. It is one of a raft of such films in Hollywood's history; from *To Sir With Love* to *Stand and Deliver* to *Dead Poets' Society*, great, inspired teachers change the lives of the young adults they teach. In this case, a young, white, beautiful ex-marine rescues Chicana/o, Mexican, African-American, and a few white students from their backgrounds by teaching them to read poetry, a favorite medium of salvation in pedagogy films. *The Substitute*, however, is a run-of-the-mill action-adventure film, whose only ideological project is to remind us that the state is incapable of discharging its responsibilities, which should be entrusted instead to mercenaries. And these differences are unmistakable in the films' very different uses of rap.

From the outset, the cueing of the first rap cut in each film marks out its ideological terrain. *The Substitute* opens with a covert mission by U.S. commandos into Cuba. As the group of operatives sits watching the newscast from which they learn that their existence will be disavowed, our hero is identified. Several members of the team express dismay and distress, but Shale (Tom Berenger) stays cool. When they ask him what to do, he answers, "Nothing. We just wait. Something will come along." While the bass line continues over a cut to an aerial view of Miami, the rap does not audibly begin until after a cut to the schoolyard. Shale is nowhere in this scene, in no way connected to the music.

Dangerous Minds, however, is organized throughout by rap. The first rap cut is the film's theme song, which begins even before the opening sequence. Coolio's "Gangsta's Paradise" introduces us to the film, the kids, and the school setting. The next musical cue begins as LouAnn (Michelle Pfeiffer) tells her buddy Hal (George Dzundza) that she has just accepted a full-time job in his school. This second rap, "Havin Thangs" by Big Mike, continues over a cut to the school yard the next day, and over another cut to LouAnn and George entering the school before fading out. LouAnn's first day is disastrous, and some music from the score by Wendy and Lisa[1] accompanies her reading teaching tips later that evening. The next morning, as she is lying in bed and has an inspiration, "Put Ya Back Into It" by Tre Black begins, and continues over a cut to the school yard, another cut into her classroom, and several shots of her preparing herself in expectation of her students' arrival.

As these scenes suggest, *The Substitute* and *Dangerous Minds* treat rap entirely differently. While rap is used to differentiate Shale from the students, it connects LouAnn and her students, drawing them together in an affective and representational world more familiar to the students than the teacher. But these insights about the films could easily be had without particular attention to the scores. Despite the many features the films share, no perceiver would be

likely to argue that Shale's relationship to his students is similar
to LouAnn's. One important insight into *Dangerous Minds*, though,
can come from considering the score.

Dangerous Minds was based on the autobiography of LouAnn
Johnson, entitled *My Posse Don't Do Homework*. Several changes in
details were made for the screenplay: Johnson's character was
made straight, and the poetry she taught was from rock instead
of rap. These are the kinds of changes for which Hollywood is
notorious, and they were noted in many reviews. Both Johnson
and her teaching techniques were homogenized, "mainstreamed"
for a mass audience. In many ways, such homogenization is an
integral part of liberal education fantasies; both teachers and students must, by the end of the films, embody liberal values such as
honesty, individualism, and appreciation of high art.[2]

In *Dangerous Minds*, however, the score opens onto identifications discouraged by these text-threads of the film. By refusing to
create and police boundaries between LouAnn Johnson and rap,
the score offers the opportunity to identify away from the most
teleological thread of the film. While it is probably not possible to
identify entirely against the notion of education as salvation, the
inclusion of Johnson in the score's hip-hop world keeps open the
possibility of multiple, shifting identifications.[3] Unlike the tight,
narrowing identifications tracked by the scores discussed in chapter 4, brief identifications with many positions and characters are
made possible by this soundtrack. In fact, the score suggests that
the major project of assimilation rests on LouAnn's shoulders,
and that she needs to learn to live in her students' world.

In this sense, *Dangerous Minds'* soundtrack moves against not only
other text-threads of the film, but also the main thrust of the
high-school-teacher-as-salvation genre. The score does not simply
support the narrative in its primacy. By moving against its central logic, it tracks identifications the film cannot control. Unlike

the ultra-nationalist identifications offered by *The Substitute* and the action-adventure films of chapter 4, *Dangerous Minds* draws LouAnn into her students' world musically. The songs group together positions, affiliate them, so that not only are there many points of entry to identification, but mobility between and among the various positions in the scenario is encouraged and made easy.

I want to turn now to another pair of films, romance films this time. Romance films have a certain logic, just as pedagogy films do. They are about unification over obstacles; the films I will discuss here take race as their primary obstacle to the romance. My purpose is again to consider how their scores work—with and against other text-threads within the film and in comparison to each other—to track their perceivers' identification processes.

Differences Attract

The release of *Mississippi Masala* in 1992 caused a great deal of stir in newspapers and cineaste circles. Its director, Mira Nair, was not only the director of the highly acclaimed *Salaam Bombay*, but also a woman of color; *Mississippi Masala* appeared at a time when there were—as has been true for most of film history—precious few women directors of any color (though this situation may be starting to change). There was a presumption of innocence on everyone's part: surely a woman of color, especially one who made a film as smart and compelling as *Salaam Bombay*, would get it right in all the ways white men, as well as the very few white women and men of color, had not. And indeed, *Mississippi Masala* briefly made Nair a mainstream director—the star-studded cast of her next feature, *The Perez Family*, included Marisa Tomei and Anjelica Huston—and left its middlebrow audiences panting for more of Denzel Washington and newcomer Sarita Choudhury.[4]

But basic knowledge of East African history, British imperial history, or Indian colonial and postcolonial history points to a problem in the film. It opens in Uganda, at the point in 1972 when General Idi Amin ordered all Asians to leave the country. It represents that moment as the insanity of Amin, and it persists throughout in representing the issue as black-against-brown racism. What is erased, what was hard to remember and impossible to see, is the status of Indians in East Africa, the distribution of wealth that created the problem, and the role England played in creating that distribution. The vast tracts of lush green fields that the family home overlooks are not simply the unspoiled Ugandan countryside, but are fields, most likely of coffee or tea, that are owned, plantation-style, by Indians and worked, exploited labor–style, by black Ugandans.

Against this backdrop of racism and erased colonial legacies, I want to look closely at how *Mississippi Masala*'s score conditions identification processes. My particular concern is to unpack how and why the film's score participates in granting Mina (Sarita Choudhury) liberal subjectivity while refusing Demetrius (Denzel Washington) any such representational rewards.

The film has two discrete kinds of music—originally composed music with a distinctively Indian flavor, and popular music, mainly African-American, ranging from New Orleans blues to new jack swing. While the African-American music produces a fantasy of community I will discuss later, I think it is important to take just a minute to describe the operations of the rest of the score. The composed portions focus on the inner psychic storms of Mina and her father Jay (Roshan Seth). Fully following contemporary Hollywood conventions, the film marks its important subjective moments with music to guide our identifications.

In one scene, for example, Mina is sitting by the motel's pool after a date that began with Harry Patel, a hot catch in the local

Indian community, and ended with Demetrius, Denzel Washington's African-American carpet cleaner. Her mother joins her poolside in the moonlight, oiling Mina's hair while they converse about what happened. Kinnu, the mother, wants desperately to hear about Harry Patel, but Mina interrupts her mother's interrogation. She asks about Okelo, the black Ugandan whom she called uncle as a child, who was part of the family and Jay's friend since childhood. Mina wants to know why Jay never contacted Okelo, why they didn't stay in touch, what happened to the deep love between them. We assume that she asks this question at this moment because she's confused about her interracial feelings toward Demetrius, an aspect of her subjective state to which her mother obviously has no access.

The music here contains many of the features Tagg (1990a) characterizes as female: slower, legato melody and accompaniment, rhythmically regular, up-down-up melodic contours, modal tonal language (see example 8). In addition, there is no strong motion, either harmonically or melodically. The instruments are few—bass, synthesized harpsichord, and flute. While the bass and harpsichord play repetitive arpeggios, the flute, which enters later, plays extended legato lines. The contemplative, slightly mournful sound articulates a mood that can only be Mina's, giving us access to her subjective state by producing its representation.

In other words, Mina's subjectivity does not exist prior to the music's representation of it, nor is it represented significantly by dialogue, acting, or visual cues. The music does not *articulate* Mina's subjectivity; it is, rather, its *only* location. In this scene, the score is the only guide for identification.

In scene after scene, the composed music does this kind of work for Mina and for Jay. There is very little Indian source music in the film—a few prayers chanted, a performance by Kinnu at a wedding. Only one instance is especially significant. On the bus ride

Example 8
Mississippi Masala: Mina and Kinnu poolside

to the Kampala airport, as the family is leaving Uganda, Kinnu is taken out by Ugandan soldiers. They force her to open her suitcase and show them the contents. They take a framed photo of Jay in full barrister's regalia and throw it in the mud. They find a piece of equipment: "What's this?" they ask; "Music." "Show me." Kinnu turns on the tape recorder, which blares "Mera Joota Hai Japani," a very popular Hindi film song. The words are:

> My shoes are Japanese,
> My pants are English,
> My red hat is Russian,
> But my heart—it's all Indian.

The song, like most Indian popular music, is from a film; this one from the Kapur film dynasty of the 1950s and 1960s. It is enormously popular and well known, and makes a clear statement about national identity in both transnational communities and a global economy.

But while *Mississippi Masala* opens with a strong sense of transnational Indian identity—undifferentiated, it is important to add, by such complications as region, language, and religion—it also undercuts any notion of a monolithic community throughout. It repeatedly marks the problems of color and class among Indians, particularly in relation to Jay and Mina. During the wedding sequence, for example, two women are discussing Harry Patel's eligibility and Kinnu's designs on him for Mina. One is worried because she wants Harry for her own daughter. The other reassures her, saying, "You can be dark and have money, or you can be fair and have no money, but you cannot be dark and have no money and expect to marry Harry Patel." The film goes out of its way, in this and many other scenes, to point to certain axes of privilege and oppression within the Indian community, but not so for the African-American.

At first glance, it might appear that Harry Patel and Alicia LeShay, Demetrius's ex-girlfriend, are parallel characters. Certainly each represents the community's pull to stay within, to marry one of your own kind. But Alicia never opens the opportunity for African Americans to criticize her—or Demetrius— parallel to the class and color discourse around Harry and Mina. Willy Ben, Demetrius's father, invites Alicia to his birthday. Tyrone, Demetrius's friend and business partner, tells Demetrius that when Demetrius gets back with Alicia, maybe he could pass Mina on to Tyrone. We are never privy to any criticism of either Alicia or Demetrius (at least, not until he is caught with Mina) from within the local African-American community.

But the single most important source of this sense of a uniform and unified community comes through the music. In the first many minutes of film time, during which Jay's theme is introduced and Kinnu's tape recorder is played, the music is composed, cued, and mixed to reflect the inner turmoil the family, especially Jay, is experiencing in leaving Uganda. Finally, as the camera pans across a map representing their journey to the United States, the composed Indian music stops over the mid-Atlantic ridge, and as Newfoundland edges into view on the left side of the screen, a driving piano-drums-bass-harmonica blues begins. This blues tune is not listed in the song credits, but it stands out from the rest of the score before and after it as a distinct song. Unmistakably, it invokes not the subjective state of an individual African American, which would be the parallel to Jay's theme, but rather a broad, historical community.

Never does the film use music to represent Demetrius or his subjective state. We first meet him a full seventeen minutes into the film, when Mina crashes into his van, in a sequence with no music. Next we see him picking up his brother Dexter from a street corner. The scene begins with the guys hanging out on the corner rapping, but no music accompanies Demetrius's entrance or his conversation with Dexter. The first time Demetrius appears with music is twenty-five minutes into the film, when he goes to pick up his father, Willie Ben, from work. The scene opens with Smiley Lewis's "Caledonia Party" blaring and a shot of Willie Ben's hands pushing a cart from curtained room to curtained room, making sure the diners have everything they need.[5] Demetrius enters about a minute later, into the storefront with the music mixed way down. The music stays mixed low as Demetrius enters the kitchen, and it continues under the rest of the scene. Nothing about this music or its cueing connects it to Demetrius.

Nor does the music of *Mississippi Masala* call attention to the subjectivity of any other African-American characters. It makes a clear distinction between music for community and atmosphere—African-American—and music for character subjectivity—Indian-influenced compositions. But the film closes with two important departures from this scheme. While Jay is in Uganda at the film's close, he goes to the school where Okelo used to teach. He learns that Okelo died not long after Jay left Uganda, killed by Amin's political forces. As Jay turns away from the school, a blues harmonica begins to play a piece of dramatic scoring (called on the CD "Sad Feeling," by Willie Cobb). There is a cut to the green fields behind his old home, and a voiceover of a letter he sends to Kinnu, renouncing his connection to Uganda and declaring his intention to come home to the United States. A cut takes us to Kinnu in her liquor store reading Jay's letter and pans across to Skillet, an older black man, playing the harmonica. Retroactively, this pan shows us that the harmonica is a kind of source scoring—simultaneously dramatic scoring in Kampala and source music in Greenwood. The music continues over a cut back to Jay walking, then fades away.

What happens in this sequence is the resolution of the work begun with the map scene at the beginning. African-American music represents not only African-American community, but America as a whole. The film projects its admirable fantasy of a warm and fuzzy community of African Americans all dancing the electric slide in tiny clubs around the country onto the entire United States. It puts African Americans at the center of U.S. life— Euro-Americans are only a shadow of oppression throughout the film. It fantasizes a community unperturbed by difference, and then projects that fantasy outward to a national scale. And the terrain of these fantasies is the film's score.

The final piece of music is even more interesting. The song, "Mundeke" by Afrigo Band, fades in as Jay walks the streets of Kampala and sees a young woman dancing in the center of a circle of onlookers. The music, a kind of Afro-Carib world-beat pop, accompanies her joyous dance, while Jay holds a black African toddler who had reached out to him. This music continues over the cut to the credits, which is intercut with shots of Demetrius and Mina dressed in kente cloth outfits twirling around in a cotton field. Just as the previous blues piece marks both Jay's connection to the United States and a particular, fantasmatic vision of it, so does this piece mark the connection between Demetrius and Mina as it routes that connection through Jay, Uganda, and the toddler—that is, through Africa.[6]

Corrina, Corrina, another 1990s interracial romance film, establishes a very different kind of musical world. Throughout the film, both the score and the dialogue go out of their way to prove to us that Corrina (Whoopi Goldberg) and Manny (Ray Liotta) share their sophisticated tastes and compelling interests in music. The first time that Corrina, the nanny, stays for dinner, "Trois Gymnopedies" is playing on the phonograph.

CORRINA: So pretty.

MANNY: Yeah. It's Eric Satie. He's a French composer.

CORRINA: Yes, I know. He was twenty-two when he wrote this. Can you imagine being so poised and having such boldness in a composition when you're only twenty-two?

Manny is clearly stunned by Corrina's musical knowledge. And the second dinner sequence is no less surprising for him:

CORRINA: Isn't that "Peace Piece"?

MANNY: Mm-hmmm.

MOLLY: My dad always listens to it.

CORRINA: I love it. You know [holding up a crystal bowl before a candle], when you listen to Bill Evans it's as though you held up a really beautifully clear crystal in front of a warm light.

MANNY: Hmmm. That's lovely. Who wrote that?

CORRINA: I did.

After dinner, the three of them watch "Name That Tune," and Corrina and Manny are fiercely competitive and equally skilled, much to Molly's amusement.

By the time of their third dinner, Manny has had the inspiration of inviting Corrina for a barbecue (her miserable cooking is one running joke of the film). When she joins Manny and Molly on the patio, Louis Armstrong's rendition of "You Go to My Head" is playing on the phonograph.

CORRINA: That's my favorite song.

MANNY: [pausing] Mine, too.

CORRINA: You know, Billie does a better version of it.

MANNY: [badly imitating Armstrong] No one's better than Louie.

Example 9
Corrina, Corrina: Jell-O Pudding jingle

After Corrina tucks Molly into bed, she helps Manny write the famous Jell-O jingle—"Who says you shouldn't / Have instant puddin'? / From J-E-L-L-O" (see example 9). And once they've polished off one of television advertising's catchiest jingles, they play a sensitive, lyrical duet together. Clearly this little musical collaboration portends great things for the joint ventures in their future.

At the level of narrative, the discussions about music and the music-making highlight the growing connection between Corrina and Manny. But they also draw our attention to the songs in the score, guaranteeing that we cannot distinguish Manny and Corrina musically. Unlike the music of *Mississippi Masala*, *Corrina, Corrina*'s score does not treat its central character and her lover differently. They share the same taste in music, right down to the same favorite song, and both are informed connoisseurs.

In the remaining romantic sequences, the same governing logic prevails. In a long intercut sequence of Manny and Corrina each on a bad date, we hear Armstrong's "You Go to My Head," which then returns during the scene in Manny's backyard where they kiss for the first time. When Corrina, Manny, and Molly fly a kite, the soundtrack is a folkie version of "Corrina, Corrina" by Ted Hawkins. Even here, identification is a fairly wide-open proposition; the song is about Corrina, but the lyrics are spoken by her lover. On no occasion does any of these songs track us into an assimilating identification.

In the only two other romantic sequences in the film, a single theme is used. Actually, this theme is first played during the scene in which Molly speaks for the first time; it has nothing to do with Manny or the romance plot. The scene begins with Molly playing the first phrase of "Good King Wenceslas" over and over—her mother had been teaching her the tune. Corrina sits down with her and fills in the missing phrase, throwing in some harmonic support for good measure. Within a few phrases, their duet becomes an orchestral endeavor that continues over a series of dissolves to Corrina doing housework in slo-mo. Molly enters as Corrina is finishing Manny's bed; the child very quietly says "Corrina? This is where my mommy sleeps." These are the first words she has spoken since her mother's funeral, and they are accompanied by the love theme in example 10.

Example 10
Corrina, Corrina: Love theme

The next time this theme is heard, it accompanies Manny coming home to find Corrina and Molly asleep together on his bed. He has bought Corrina the album on which Louis Armstrong and Oscar Peterson play "You Go to My Head" as a thank-you gift for her help with the Jell-O pudding jingle. Later, Manny takes Molly and Corrina out to dinner, their first public outing as a "family."

The final appearance of the love theme is the film's penultimate scene. Manny has tried to apologize to Corrina, and she has turned him away. With a cut to a long shot of Manny looking skyward, attempting to talk to a God he has never believed in, we hear the love theme.

The music in this cycle of three scenes serves as a kind of backbone for the identification processes the film offers. We begin the film with an identification with Molly, who openly gives her love to Corrina early on, and then offers Corrina to her father, who first loves the Corrina who curls up with Molly on the bed, but ultimately also the Corrina who rejects him. Retrospectively, this pattern makes sense of the music in the early part of the film, almost all of which speaks for Molly.

In scoring the romantic scenes between Mina and Demetrius, *Mississippi Masala* makes some very different choices than *Corrina, Corrina*. First, there are many more scenes between Demetrius and Mina than between Manny and Corrina—seven more, to be exact—and there is hardly any consistency in musical style:

- First dance, in the Leopard Lounge—Keith Sweat, "Just One of Them Thangs"
- Chinese restaurant—pseudo-Chinese source music
- In van as Demetrius drives Mina to meet his family—Delta blues, slide steel guitar
- Bayou—no music, first kiss

- At motel reception desk—no music
- On the phone—no music
- On bus to Biloxi—harmonica blues, begin in bus, continue under conversation
- Beach at sunset—no music
- Ferris wheel—carnival music
- Making love in motel—African music "Kanda Ya Nini" by The Papy Tex Group
- Waking up in motel—Jay's theme
- Mina chases Demetrius in car—percussion, African-influenced
- Demetrius to Mina—"I never thought I'd fall in love with you"—Jay's theme
- Demetrius tells Willie Ben he's leaving—blues guitar
- Mina tells Kinnu she's leaving—Jay's theme
- Final Song—"Mundeke" by Afrigo Band

Certainly, some tendencies appear in this list. In particular, the blues, African pop, and the absence of music would be important groups of musical cues to consider in an extended analysis of the film. But I am most interested in the three scenes between Mina and Demetrius that are scored with Jay's theme.

Example 11
Mississippi Masala: Jay's theme

Throughout the first half-hour, this theme accompanies Jay. First, it plays as Okelo drops Jay off at home, across a cut to

Jay sitting on his patio, weeping as he surveys the lush fields of the homeland he has just decided to leave. Next, it accompanies Jay, Kinnu, and Mina as they drive away. We then hear the theme as they line up on the tarmac at the Kampala airport to leave Uganda forever, and it continues over the cut to the map and the pan from Uganda across Africa to the Atlantic, where it gives way to the hard, Chicago-style blues discussed earlier.

In this way, Jay's theme is strongly connected with Uganda. And, not surprisingly, it is not heard again until Jay reads the letter from the High Court in Kampala informing him of the date for his hearing. After reading the letter, he goes to see Kinnu in her store, and his theme underscores their conversation:

JAY: From where to where we've come, Kinnu?
KINNU: No point thinking like that.
   [Jay walks over and sits down.]
KINNU: [raising a glass to Jay] Here's to your lawsuit.
JAY: (Says something, presumably in their native language.)
   Cheers.
KINNU: Cheers.

He does not tell Kinnu about the letter, but Jay's theme reminds us that Uganda is really the topic on his mind.

The theme next appears when Mina has a nightmare about Uganda and awakens sobbing in Demetrius's arms. As he soothes her, we hear Jay's theme. This time, however, it is played on solo guitar; the soundtrack album identifies this as the "Love Theme." At this moment, Jay's theme in the guitar orchestration makes links among Jay, Uganda, Mina, and Demetrius.

The original associations and orchestration of the theme return when it plays during a flashback of Okelo telling Jay that "Africa is for Africans ... Black Africans." It continues over a cut to an aerial shot of the motel exterior and then to Jay asking Mina, "Do you know why we left Uganda?" Several scenes later, we hear it when Jay tells Kinnu they are returning to Uganda. As he says, "Kinnu, we are getting old ... I don't want to die in some strangers' country," his theme enters in its original orchestration.

But then the problems that began with Mina's nightmare are compounded even further. When Demetrius tells Mina, "I never thought I'd fall in love with you," we hear Jay's theme yet again in the solo guitar version from the nightmare scene. The final instance of Jay's theme occurs when Mina calls home to tell her parents that she cannot go to Uganda, that she is going away with Demetrius. It enters at the end of the conversation, as she says, "Kiss Papa for me," continues over the cut to Demetrius and Mina in the phone booth, and over the cut to Kinnu explaining Mina's behavior to Jay. In this way, Jay, his relationship to Uganda, and the relationship between Mina and Demetrius are all inextricably intertwined.

One might compare the love theme from *Corrina, Corrina* to Jay's theme. In each case, the music builds a relationship between father and daughter and between lovers. In each case, the theme shifts over the course of the film, avoiding the tight regulation of scores offering assimilating identifications. But I want to suggest that a more subtle comparison of these themes is possible. The love theme offers an affiliation of sorts between Molly and Manny in terms of their attachments to Corrina. The historical conditions of racism are spoken at the surface of the film, and nothing suggests equivalence or translatability of experience across lines of race. For example, a few lines later in the Bill Evans–accompanied dinner scene, Manny asks Corrina if she has ever tried to write poetry or liner notes. She answers dryly that, "Basically, they just let us play the music; they don't let us write about it." Jay's theme, however, levels a number of distinct historical conditions (racism and postcoloniality in Uganda, racism and immigration in the American South, the varying imbrications of race and class in both places) in order to route a non-race-based connection between Mina and Demetrius through Africa.

Identifications and Identities

Of the four films I have discussed in this chapter, only *The Substitute* engages in assimilating identifications. Even *Mississippi Masala*, for all its musical distinctions between Mina and Demetrius, does not track perceivers quite so narrowly into a singular identification.

This difference, I want to suggest, is at the center of how scores work. Scores in the classical Hollywood tradition, whether or not they particularly use the symphonic musical materials of that tradition, track perceivers into assimilating identifications. While not every score uses the same musical materials or scoring techniques to achieve these identifications, the end result is still the same. We are quite tightly tracked into identification with a single subject position that does not challenge dominant ideologies.

No film can force a perceiver to engage in a particular way. Even the most rigidly assimilating of film scores cannot guarantee the cooperation of perceiving subjects. We may well opt out of engagement altogether, or we may be delighted (against all odds and along with the inhabitants of a homeless shelter described in Fiske [1993]) at the destruction of the good guys. But such resistances should not be taken to mean that any identification is plausible in any film.

The scores of films like *Dangerous Minds* and *Corrina, Corrina* track our identifications too. They simply do not do so as rigidly or unidirectionally. *Dangerous Minds* encourages identifications with particular students—especially Callie and Raoul—at various moments. *Corrina, Corrina* tracks our identifications toward Molly early in the film, subsequently steering them more and more toward Corrina. *Bagdad Cafe* moves our identifications back and forth between Brenda and Jasmin.

Such identifications-in-process might best be called *affiliating,* a term I introduced earlier. Rather than assimilating perceivers into one particular subject position, these identifications make affiliations that do not require absorption of one subject into another position. Unlike assimilating identifications, affiliating identifications can accommodate axes of identity and the conditions of subjectivity they create. They can permit resistances and allow multiple and mobile identifications.

And they depend quite heavily on films' scores. We can identify with several positions over the course of *Dangerous Minds* precisely because the score does not limit its main musical materials to one character or group of characters. Both "I Am Calling You" and the ragtime theme in *Bagdad Cafe* connect us to Brenda and Jasmin as a unit and to the world they create around them, not to one or the other. And *Corrina, Corrina* tells us, at the level of narrative, that we should not associate "You Go to My Head" with either Manny or Corrina, but rather with them both. In each case, the score is the condition of possibility for these affiliating identifications—it opens opportunities for perceivers and our histories that scores offering assimilating identifications work very hard to foreclose.

Tracking Identifications
An Epilogue

Throughout this book, I have made the case that the identifications perceivers engage in depend centrally on music. In any discussion of how films participate in producing identity formations, the challenge is to describe the engagements between films and perceivers. That cannot plausibly be done without examining the score. And when I say "examine the score," I do not mean, as I have shown throughout the preceding chapters, a simple textual analysis. Rather, any consideration of how scores track identifications must include considerations of both perceiver and music histories.

Not all scores, I have argued, track identifications similarly. Assimilating and affiliating identifications do not share much in the way of processes or methods. Their relations with perceivers function in structurally distinct ways. Assimilating identifications track perceivers toward a rigid, tightly controlled position that tends to line up comfortably with aspects of dominant ideologies. Affiliating identifications track perceivers toward a more loosely defined position that groups, or affiliates, several different narrative positions within a fantasy scenario together. In other words, it is not simply that assimilating identification is one and affiliating is several. More than numbers, the difference is one of direction: assimilating identifications narrow or tighten possibilities, while affiliating identifications open outward.

But affiliating identifications are also less tidy, somehow, than assimilating identifications. Like an unruly child, a perceiver engaged in affiliating identification doesn't stay in one place; at any given moment, you cannot be sure where to find her. Whether a perceiver identifies with Jasmin or Brenda in a particular scene of *Bagdad Cafe* will depend on many factors: textual factors, such as camera angle and music, to be sure, but also the perceiver's own psychic formations and histories. In this sense, no theory can fully predict identifications, and no text can guarantee them. But scores that track perceivers toward affiliating identifications don't try to make such a guarantee. And for this reason, I imagine I will continue to prefer scores and films that track me towards affiliating identifications.

The technical features of film scores—from musical materials to cueing to mixing—that are associated with these different kinds of identification offers are also different. Scores associated with assimilating identifications tend to use classical Hollywood materials and procedures, while affiliating identifications are more often associated with other musical materials, compiled scores, and less discreet cueing and mixing (see, for example, the comparison in chapter 5 of the opening sequences of *Dangerous Minds* and *The Substitute*). If this tendency continues over time, then the musical materials themselves will begin to accrue meanings accordingly. As these semiotic values adhere to musical sounds, the relationships of musics and listeners will alter, and such shifts will demand close attention in both film and music studies.

However, it is not the case that certain kinds of music *necessarily* track us into either affiliating or assimilating identifications, as the example of *The Substitute* clearly shows. The tendencies are important, and I hope future scholarship on film music will explore their ramifications. But no music can guarantee one or the other kind of identification. First, scores and their films can only make offers—identification depends on a perceiver's engagement for its very existence. Any score and its film can only play a probability game: in creating a set of conditions, some engagements are made more likely than others. But no matter what direction the score takes, toward assimilating or affiliating identifications, the process will not engage all perceivers. The score's offer will sometimes fail to be taken up.

Second, any music can be set in a context in which it can do unlikely psychic and ideological work. In chapter 3, I argued that *Dangerous Liaisons* depended on Baroque music to track identifications with the Marquise de Merteuil, while both *Desert Hearts* and *Thelma and Louise* use country music. Neither Baroque nor country music on their own terms appear to be either feminist or feminine, yet they fulfill such functions in these films. On the flip side, as it were, the fusion-based scores for the *Lethal Weapon* films track perceivers into assimilating identifications, even though the history of fusion as a genre might make that direction seem unlikely. The musical genre contributes to the offers a score makes, as I have suggested, but how it is cued and mixed, for example, can make a very big difference.

I have been tempted all along to assign a different, and specifically higher, value to affiliating identifications. They are certainly more appealing to me, because they offer more possibilities for perceivers' historically constituted subjectivities than assimilating identifications do. But such assignments of value are by no means simple or clear. As I suggested above, scores, including those that offer affiliating identifications, cannot guarantee that perceivers will engage in their offers. Nor do they offer an unlimited array of identifications. There is little risk, for example, that any perceiver will engage in significant identifications with the vice-principal or principal of the school in *Dangerous Minds*. Its score offers a range of possibilities, but that range is not infinite.

It might seem that scores that offer affiliating identifications are more socially progressive or aesthetically innovative, whatever one might mean by such phrases. But *Dangerous Minds* and *Corrina, Corrina* are unlikely to be remembered as great films, and they are susceptible to critique as liberal pluralist fantasies of the most obvious kind.[1] To stay a bit longer with *Dangerous Minds*, the most interesting feature of its score for this study is that the affiliating identifications it offers contradict, in many ways, the dominant ideological thread of the narrative. While the story most clearly offers itself to be read as an education-is-the-only-salvation parable of class mobility, the score suggests a different trajectory. Without LouAnn's willingness to enter into the world of the students, the students could not have accepted anything she had to offer. In this way, *Dangerous Minds* stands out from other true-story pedagogy films, such as *Lean on Me* (1989) and *Stand and Deliver* (1988), and the difference is performed most centrally in the score. Nonetheless, the most readily available understanding of *Dangerous Minds* hears it as the fantasy of an American dream in hip-hop beat. (This may not simply be a matter of features of the text. Pedagogy films, both this group of "true stories" and others like *Dead Poets' Society* and *Renaissance Man*, as a genre perform the liberal pluralist fantasies that anyone with sufficient education can be class mobile. That generic tendency makes it difficult to read any individual film differently.) Scores—like that of *Dangerous Minds*—that track affiliating identifications may not be working in the same directions as other aspects of the film. Thus, my point is not that affiliating identifications are somehow necessarily *better* than assimilating identifications. Any form of identification can do any kind of social or aesthetic work.

Not all multiple identifications are simply affiliating, however. *The Mask of Zorro* (1998), for example, is a film in which identifications necessarily shift from the old Zorro (Anthony Hopkins) to the new (Antonio Banderas). In many ways, there is nothing new about this score or its film. The music was composed by James Horner, who has composed more than seventy scores over twenty years, ranging from *The Dresser* (1983) to *An American Tail* (1986) to *Braveheart* (1995). Its style is fairly predictable and heavy-handed, using several leitmotivs throughout, lots of one-time dramatic scoring, references to Spanish (not Mexican) music, and music in almost every scene (well over 50 percent of the film time).

Over the course of the film, the role of Zorro shifts from Diego de la Vega (Hopkins) to Alejandro Murrieta (Banderas). The amount of screen time, the camera angles, and editing all switch balance from one to the other. But the change takes place most vividly, and most blatantly, I suggest, in the score. The theme appears some twenty-four times throughout the film.[2] The first ten occurrences accompany Diego, both before his imprisonment and after he becomes Alejandro's instructor.

The first time Zorro's theme appears with Alejandro is the first time he appears as Zorro. Without Diego's blessing, he puts on a black scarf and steals a black Andalusian horse. As he leaps onto the horse, we hear Zorro's theme. Even though he fumbles through this sequence, and even though Diego later whips Alejandro's "mask" off, Zorro's theme accompanies Alejandro then and for the rest of the film. It never again accompanies Diego, not even when he is fighting his archenemy, Don Rafael Montero (Stuart Wilson II), nor when he is dying. There is a brief, partial (two-measure) statement of the theme as Montero puts a gun to the neck of Elena (Catherine Zeta-Jones), reminding us that this enmity began when Diego was still Zorro. But fundamentally, the identity of Zorro is never shared—once Alejandro becomes Zorro, he is the only Zorro.

There are several other themes in the film:

- Elena's theme;
- the theme from the song "I Want to Spend My Lifetime Loving You," which pairs Diego and his daughter, Elena;
- "Malaguena," a familiar theme that signifies Spain and Spanishness that was composed by Cuban Ernesto Lecuona, and that accompanies much of the swordplay.

All of this music performs a little sleight of hand regarding various Latin identities. While Diego is the Spanish nobleman, Alejandro is a Californian peasant, yet he fights to "Malaguena," and in the closing sequence he is treated with the remaining three themes over the course of just a few minutes. By becoming Zorro, it would seem, Alejandro also acquires new class and national identities as well.

Since the focus of the score shifts from character to character, it might at first seem to track us toward affiliating identifications. But in no case does the score encourage multiple possible identifications within a given musical cue. Rather, the Zorro theme keeps us firmly located with Alejandro, while the "Lifetime" theme occurs a handful of times, reestablishing a sentimental bond with Diego. In the very final shot, as Alejandro walks away from the camera, he is accompanied by the "Lifetime" theme for the first time. Only now, after Diego's death, can Elena be transferred to Alejandro, making his transition to his new class, national, and secret identities complete. Such rigid tracking is the hallmark of scores that offer assimilating identifications.

The relationship between identities and identification is never obvious, textually or for perceivers. Perceivers identify away from their identities all the time—this is the fundamental assumption of scores that offer assimilating identifications. But the discourses of identity have shifted significantly throughout the 1980s and

1990s. One way to tell the story of those shifts is to say that more people living in nondominant identities are unwilling to identify away from them than ever before.

The best snapshot of this in film may come from *Philadelphia*. During her testimony, the character played by Anna Deveare Smith says:

> Mr. Wheeler's secretary, Lydia, said that Mr. Wheeler had a problem with my earrings. Apparently, Mr. Wheeler felt that they were too ... "ethnic," is the word she used, and she told me that he said that he would like it if I wore something a little less garish, a little smaller, and more "American." I said, "My earrings are American. They're *African* American."

She suggests, in other words, that she is unwilling to identify, through her clothing choices, with whiteness. People now more frequently wear fashions associated with their subcultures or heritages; there are more demands for inclusive hiring and representational practices; more and more vocal criticism is leveled at negative and stereotypical portrayals of nondominant groups. Along lines of sexuality, race, gender, ethnicity, and disability, lived cultures have learned to frown on assimilation in the past two decades.

This is, of course, the result of long, long processes of social and political struggle, not some fly-by-night recent development. But the presence of such issues in mainstream discourses skyrocketed in the 1980s, to the extent that it provoked the now all-too-familiar phenomena of the men's movement, the growth of right-wing militias, "angry white men," attacks on affirmative action, the rise in anti-gay hate crimes, and so on (for scholarship on these shifts in the material and discursive terrains, see Faludi 1991; Berlant 1997; Joseph 1996; Kintz and Lesage 1998; Fenster 1999). These responses look to protect an identity formation as old as the

U.S. Constitution: liberal pluralist in discourse, materially white, property-owning, heterosexual, and male.

The struggles between these competing visions of identity, I suspect, are intimately tied to the prevalence of scores that offer both assimilating and affiliating identifications on the contemporary film musical landscape. In other words, these two different kinds of identification parallel quite precisely the two perspectives on identity I just described. I chose to work on films of this period with at first only a barely formed sense that they would somehow present different theoretical issues than those of Hollywood's classical period. And that sense served me well—scores of the 1980s and 1990s present different theoretical challenges precisely because they come from a different social historical context, one that is remade and reproduced in score after score, not least the dozen analyzed in the second section of this book.

Scores alone do not condition the engagements between perceivers and films. I have argued throughout *Hearing Film*, however, that it is one of their primary functions, and that identifications in film depend on scores as much as, if not more than, aspects of film that have been more routinely subjected to theorizing and criticism. In order for the scholarly attention to identities that has developed in the 1990s to account for processes of identity formation, attempts to understand the relationship between identity and identification must grow and develop. Without beginning to hear the soundtracks of our stories—whether on film, television, audio books, or interactive media—that task will be impossible.

Appendix A
Four Tables of Data from Tagg and Clarida,
Ten Little Title Tunes

In 1989, I spent a semester working with Philip Tagg on his research with Robert Clarida on film and television theme music semiotics. Below are four tables of data I compiled and organized from their research on how their listeners heard some of the groundbreaking questions raised by feminist theory. See chapter 1 for a discussion of the Tagg and Clarida study and these tables.

Table 1: The Nature/Culture Dichotomy

Category	Average Percent Occurrence	
	Female	Male
Outdoors	0.96	0.42
Indoors	0.84	8.39
Clubs	0.21	7.11
Secluded Spot	0.67	0.00
Cars	0.46	9.23
Rural	27.38	2.35
Urban	2.28	16.87
Weather	7.64	1.20
Seasons	4.21	0.30

Table 2: The Mobile/Immobile Dichotomy

Category	Average Percent Occurrence	
	Female	Male
Reflection	4.29	0.17
Stasis	2.77	0.75
Dynamism	3.73	11.30
Culturally emergent	0.00	4.82
Destiny	4.73	0.00
Against will of	3.92	0.00
Stationary acts	1.54	0.33
Conflictive	0.46	3.52
Transferential	0.13	7.89

Table 3: The Male/Not-Male Dichotomy

Category	Total Per mil Occurrence	Order of Frequency
One male	99.6	2
Several people	90.5	5
Several males	42.9	20
One person	39.3	23
Couple	31.4	28
One female	22.3	40
Many people	13.4	66
Several females	7.7	94
Two persons	7.3	98

Table 4: The Private/Public Dichotomy

Category	Average Percent Occurrence	
	Female	Male
Tranquillity	4.42	0.03
Stasis	2.77	0.75
Strength	0.09	1.27
Asociality	0.00	1.65
Love	21.79	0.88
Cars	0.46	9.23
Weapons	0.00	0.30
Festive	0.21	2.67
Presentational	0.36	11.87
Military	0.04	2.84

Appendix B

"Childhood's Street" ("Barndommens gade")
Tove Ditlevsen, 1942

I am the street of your childhood,
I am the root of your ways.
I am the throbbing rhythm
in everything you may desire.

I am your mother's gray hands
and your father's worried mind,
and I am the light, wispy yarn
of your earliest dreams.

I gave you my great seriousness
one day when you were lost,
and I drizzled a little melancholy in
your mind one night in the driving rain.

I hit you once to the ground
to make your heart hard,
but I gently pulled you up again
and dried the tears away.

It was I that taught you to hate,
and I taught you hardness and cruelty.

I gave you the strongest weapons,
you must know how to use them well.

I gave you those watchful eyes,
by them shall you be known again,
and if you meet someone with the same look,
you will know he is your friend.

Did you fly so far over countries,
did you grow away from your friend?
I am the street of your childhood,
I always know you again.

This text appeared in 1942 in a collection entitled *Lille Verden* (little world) published by Athenæum in Copenhagen; the translation is mine. It is often made slightly gentler in song versions; while the final line of the poem suggests the impossibility of escape (similar to, for example, The Eagles' "You can check out any time you like, but you can never leave"), Anne Linnett's song version, for example, uses its musical elements and careful editing of the text to push the sense toward stability and security.

Appendix C
Box Office Receipts (in millions)
as of April 27, 1999, for Films Discussed

Film title	Domestic	Overseas	Worldwide Total
Bagdad Cafe (1988) (aka *Out of Rosenheim*)	$3.6	—	$3.6
Corrina, Corrina (1994)	20.2	—	20.2
Dangerous Liaisons (1988)	34.7	—	34.7
Dangerous Minds (1995)	84.9	93	177.9
Desert Hearts (1985)	2.5	—	2.5
Dirty Dancing (1987)	63.9	106.4	170.3
The Hunt for Red October (1990)	120.7	78.5	199.2
Indiana Jones and the Temple of Doom (1984)	179.9	153.2	333.1
Lethal Weapon 2 (1989)	147.3	80	227.3
Mississippi Masala (1991)	7.3	—	7.3
The Mask of Zorro (1998)	93.8	139.6	233.4
The Substitute (1996)	14.8	—	14.8
Thelma and Louise (1991)	45.4	—	45.4

Taken from Chuck Kahn's Movie Page on the Internet at
www.vex.net/~odin/Gross.

Works Cited

Adorno, Theodor. (1988). *Introduction to the Sociology of Music.* New York: Continuum.

Althusser, Louis. (1971). "Ideology and Ideological State Apparatuses," in *Lenin and Philosophy,* trans. Ben Brewster. New York: Monthly Review Press, pp. 121–73.

Altman, Charles F. (1980). "Introduction," *Yale French Studies* 6, pp. 3–15.

Anderson, Benedict. (1981). *Imagined Communities: Reflections on the Origin and Spread of Nationalism.* New York: Verso.

Anderson, Gillian. (1987). "The Presentation of Silent Films, or, Music as Anaesthesia," *Journal of Musicology* 5, 2 (Spring), pp. 257–95.

Anzaldúa, Gloria. (1987). *Borderlands/La Frontera: The New Mestiza.* San Francisco: Aunt Lute Books.

Anzieu, Didier. (1974). "L'envelope sonore du soi," *Revue française de psychanalyse* 37, no. 1: 161–79.

Appel, Willi and Ralph T. Daniel. (1960). *The Harvard Brief Dictionary of Music.* New York: Pocket Books.

Axelsen, Jens. (1984). *Dansk-engelsk Ordbog.* Copenhagen: Gyldendalske Boghandel.

Barthes, Roland. (1977). "The Death of the Author," in *Image/Music/Text,* trans. Stephen Heath. New York: Hill and Wang, pp. 142–48.

Bazelon, Irwin. (1975). *Knowing the Score.* New York: Van Nostrand Reinhold.

Bergeron, Katherine and Philip V. Bohlman (Eds.) (1992). *Disciplining Music: Musicology and Its Canons.* Chicago: University of Chicago Press.

Bergstrom, Janet and Mary Ann Doane. (1990). "Introduction," *Camera Obscura* 20–21 (special issue on "The Spectatrix"), pp. 5–27.

Berlant, Lauren. (1997). *The Queen of America Goes to Washington City: Essays on Sex and Citizenship.* Durham, NC: Duke University Press.

Bordwell, David and Kristin Thompson. (1993). *Film Art: An Introduction.* New York : McGraw-Hill (4th edition).

Brackett, David. (1995). *Interpreting Popular Music.* New York and Cambridge: Cambridge University Press.

Bradby, Barbara. (1990). "Do Talk and Don't Talk," in Simon Frith and Andrew Goodwin (Eds.), *On Record: Rock, Pop, and the Written Word.* New York: Pantheon Books, pp. 341–68.

Bradley, Dick, "The Cultural Study of Music," Stenciled occasional paper, Centre for Contemporary Cultural Studies (University of Birmingham, England), General Series SP No. 61.

Brett, Philip. (1994). "Musicality, Essentialism, and the Closet," in Philip Brett, Elizabeth Wood, and Gary C. Thomas (Eds.), *Queering the Pitch: The New Gay and Lesbian Musicology.* New York and London: Routledge.

Brett, Philip, Elizabeth Wood, and Gary C. Thomas (Eds.) (1994). *Queering the Pitch: The New Gay and Lesbian Musicology.* New York and London: Routledge.

Brown, Royal S. (1994). *Overtones and Undertones: Reading Film Music.* Berkeley: University of California Press.

Butler, Judith. (1990). *Gender Trouble: Feminism and the Subversion of Identity.* New York: Routledge.

Camera Obscura. (1990). 20–21, special issue on "The Spectatrix."

Certeau, Michel de. (1984). *The Practice of Everyday Life,* trans. Steven F. Rendall. Berkeley: University of California Press.

Clifford, James. (1988). *The Predicament of Culture: Twentieth-Century Ethnography, Literature, and Art.* Cambridge, MA: Harvard University Press.

Clifford, James and George E. Marcus. (1986). *Writing Culture: The Poetics and Politics of Ethnography.* Berkeley: University of California Press.

Clough, Patricia Ticineto. (1992). *The End(s) of Ethnography: From Realism to Social Criticism.* Newbury Park, CA: Sage.

Collins, Jim, Hilary Radner, and Ava Preacher Collins (Eds.) (1993). *Film Theory Goes to the Movies.* New York: Routledge.

Cooke, Deryck. (1959). *The Language of Music.* Oxford and New York: Oxford University Press. (Reprinted in 1963, 1989, 1990.)

Crary, Jonathan. (1990). *Techniques of the Observer: On Vision and Modernity in the Nineteenth Century.* Cambridge, MA: MIT Press.

Cubitt, Sean. (1984). "Maybellene: Meaning and the Listening Subject," *Popular Music* 4, pp. 207–24.

Doane, Mary Ann. (1980a). "Ideology and the Practice of Sound Editing and Mixing," in Stephen Heath and Theresa de Lauretis (Eds.), *The Cinematic Apparatus*. London: Macmillan, pp. 47–56.

———. (1980b). "The Voice in the Cinema: The Articulation of Body and Space," *Yale French Studies* 60, pp. 33–50.

———. (1987). *The Desire to Desire: The Woman's Film of the 1940s*. Bloomington: Indiana University Press.

Doane, Mary Ann, Patricia Mellencamp, and Linda Williams (Eds.). (1984). *Re-Vision: Essays in Feminist Film Criticism*. Frederick, MD: University Publications of America.

Eisler, Hanns and Theodor Adorno. (1947). *Composing for the Films*. New York: Oxford University Press. (Reprinted 1994. London: Athlone Press.)

Esslin, Martin. (1980). *Brecht: A Choice of Evils*. London: Eyre Methuen.

Ewen, Elizabeth. (1985). *Immigrant Women in the Land of Dollars: Life and Culture on the Lower East Side, 1890–1925*. New York: Monthly Review Press.

Ewen, Stuart and Elizabeth Ewen. (1992). *Channels of Desire: Mass Images and the Shaping of American Consciousness*. Minneapolis: University of Minnesota Press.

Fabbri, Franco. (1982). "A Theory of Musical Genres: Two Applications," in David Horn and Philip Tagg (Eds.), *Popular Music Perspectives*. Göteborg and Exeter: IASPM, pp. 52–81.

Faludi, Susan. (1991). *Backlash: The Undeclared War against American Women*. New York: Crown.

Fenster, Mark. (1999). *Conspiracy Theories: Secrecy and Power in American Culture*. Minneapolis: University of Minnesota Press.

Fink, Robert. (2000). "Orchestral Corporate," in *Echo: A Music-Centered Journal*. University of California at Los Angeles.

Fiske, John. (1982). *Introduction to Communication Studies*. New York: Methuen.

———. (1987). "British Cultural Studies and Television," in Robert C. Allen (Ed.), *Channels of Discourse*. Chapel Hill: University of North Carolina Press, pp. 254–89.

———. (1993). *Power Plays, Power Works*. New York and London: Verso.

Flinn, Caryl. (1986a). "Sound, Woman and the Bomb: Dismembering the 'Great Whatsit' in Kiss Me Deadly," *Wide Angle* 8, 3/4, pp. 115–27.

————. (1986b). "The 'Problem' of Femininity in Theories of Film Music," *Screen* 27, 6, pp. 56–72.

————. (1992). *Strains of Utopia: Gender, Nostalgia, and Hollywood Film Music.* Princeton, NJ: Princeton University Press.

Foucault, Michel. (1972). *The Archaeology of Knowledge,* trans. A. M. Sheridan. New York: Pantheon Books.

————. (1979). "What Is an Author," in Josué V. Harari (Ed.), *Textual Strategies: Perspectives in Post-Structuralist Criticism.* Ithaca, NY: Cornell University Press, pp. 141–60.

Frith, Simon. (1981). *Sound Effects: Youth, Leisure, and the Politics of Rock 'n' Roll.* New York: Pantheon Books.

————. (1984). "Mood Music: An Inquiry into Narrative Film Music," in *Screen* 25, 3 (May-June), (special issue "On the Soundtrack"), pp. 78–87.

Frith, Simon and Angela McRobbie. (1990). "Rock and Sexuality," in Simon Frith and Andrew Goodwin (Eds.), *On Record: Rock, Pop, and the Written Word.* New York: Pantheon Books, pp. 371–89.

Gallez, Douglas. (1970). "Theories of Film Music," *Cinema Journal* 9, 2 (Spring), pp. 40–47.

Gelpi, Barbara. (1992). *Shelley's Goddess: Maternity, Language, Subjectivity.* New York: Oxford University Press.

Gilbert, Sandra M. and Susan Gubar. (1979). *The Madwoman in the Attic: The Woman Writer and the Nineteenth-Century Literary Imagination.* New Haven, CT: Yale University Press.

Gilroy, Paul. (1987). *"There Ain't No Black in the Union Jack": The Cultural Politics of Race and Nation.* London: Hutchinson.

Giroux, Henry A. (1993). "Reclaiming the Social: Pedagogy, Resistance, and Politics in Celluloid Culture," in Jim Collins, Hillary Radner, and Ava Preacher Collins (Eds.), *Film Theory Goes to the Movies.* New York: Routledge.

Glasser, Theodore L. and James S. Ettema. (1989). "Investigative Journalism and the Moral Order" in *Critical Studies in Mass Communication* 6, pp. 1–20.

Gledhill, Christine. (1987). *Home Is where the Heart Is: Studies in Melodrama and the Woman's Film.* London: British Film Institute.

Gorbman, Claudia. (1987). *Unheard Melodies: Narrative Film Music.* Bloomington and Indianapolis: Indiana University Press.

Grossberg, Lawrence. (1992). *We Gotta Get out of This Place: Popular Conservatism and Postmodern Culture.* New York: Routledge.

Grout, Donald and Claude Palisca. (1988). *A History of Western Music.* New York: W. W. Norton.

Hacker, Andrew. (1992). *Two Nations: Black and White, Separate, Hostile, Unequal.* New York: Scribner's.

Hagen, Earle. (1971). *Scoring for Films; a Complete Text.* New York: Criterion Music Corp.

Hall, Stuart. (1980). "Encoding/Decoding," in Hall, Hobson, Lowe and Willis (Eds.), *Culture, Media, Language.* London: Hutchinson, pp. 128–39.

———. (1990). "The Emergence of Cultural Studies and the Crisis of the Humanities," *October* 53, pp. 11–23.

Hansen, Miriam. (1986). "Pleasure, Ambivalence, Identification: Valentino and Female Spectatorship," *Cinema Journal* 25, 4, pp. 6–32.

Haskell, Molly. (1974). *From Reverence to Rape: The Treatment of Women in the Movies.* New York: Holt, Rinehart, and Winston, 1974. (1987, Chicago: University of Chicago Press.)

Jaggar, Alison M. (1983). *Feminist Politics and Human Nature.* Totowa, NJ: Rowman & Allanheld.

Jhally, Sut and Justin Lewis. (1992). *Enlightened Racism: The Cosby Show, Audiences, and the Myth of the American Dream.* Boulder, CO: Westview Press.

Johnson, Richard. (1987). "What Is Cultural Studies Anyway?," *Social Text* 16 (Winter), pp. 38–80.

Jones, Steven G. (1992). *Rock Formation: Technology, Music and Mass Communication.* Newbury Park, CA: Sage.

———. (Ed.). (1997). *Virtual Culture: Identity and Communication in Cybersociety.* Newbury Park, CA: Sage.

Joseph, Miranda. (1996). "The Perfect Moment: Christians, Gays, and the National Endowment for the Arts," *Socialist Review* 26, pp. 3–4.

Kalinak, Kathryn. (1982). "The Fallen Woman and the Virtuous Wife: Musical Stereotypes in *The Informer, Gone with the Wind*, and *Laura*," *Film Reader* 5, pp. 76–82.

———. (1992). *Settling the Score.* Madison: University of Wisconsin Press.

Kaplan, E. Ann (Ed.). (1978). *Women in Film Noir.* London: British Film Institute.

Kassabian, Anahid. (1997). "At the Twilight's Last Scoring," in David Schwarz, Anahid Kassabian, and Lawrence Siegel (Eds.), *Keeping Score: Music, Disciplinarity, Culture.* Charlottesville: University Press of Virginia.

————. (1994). "A Woman Scored," in Norman Denzin (Ed.), *Studies in Symbolic Interaction* 15, 1, JAI Press.

————. (Ed.). (1993). *"and the walls come a-tumblin' down: Music in the Age of Postdisciplinarity."* Special issue (vol. 3, no. 2) of *Stanford Humanities Review.*

Kellner, Douglas and Michael Ryan. (1988). *Camera Politica: The Politics and Ideology of Contemporary Hollywood Film.* Bloomington: Indiana University Press.

King, Norman. (1984). "The Sounds of Silents," *Screen* 25, 3 (May-June), (special issue "On the Soundtrack"), pp. 2–15.

Kintz, Linda and Julia Lesage (Eds.) (1998). *Media, Culture, and the Religious Right.* Minneapolis: University of Minneapolis.

Kivy, Peter. (1990). *Music Alone: Philosophical Reflections on the Purely Musical Experience.* Ithaca, NY: Cornell University Press.

————. (1993). *The Fine Art of Repetition: Essays in the Philosophy of Music.* New York: Cambridge University Press.

Kramer, Lawrence. (1990). *Music as Cultural Practice.* Berkeley: University of California Press.

Kuhn, Annette. (1982). *Women's Pictures: Feminism and Cinema.* Boston: Routledge and Kegan Paul.

Lacombe, Alain and Claude Roclé. (1979). *La Musique du film.* Paris: F. van de Velde.

Lant, Antonia. (1991). *Blackout.* Princeton, NJ: Princeton University Press.

Lauretis, Teresa de. (1984). "Desire in Narrative," in *Alice Doesn't: Feminism, Semiotics, Cinema.* Bloomington: Indiana University Press.

Leeuwen, Theo van. (1988). "Music and Ideology: Notes toward a Sociosemiotics of Mass Media Music," Sydney Association for Studies in Culture and Society, Working Papers Series 2, 1.

Leppert, Richard and Susan McClary (Eds.). (1987). *Music and Society: The Politics of Composition, Performance, and Reception.* Cambridge: Cambridge University Press.

Levin, Tom. (1984). "The Acoustic Dimension: Notes on Cinema Sound," *Screen* 25, 3 (May-June), (special issue "On the Soundtrack"), pp. 55–68.

Lissa, Zofia. (1965). *Ästhetik der Filmmusik.* Berlin, DDR: Henschelverlag. (Originally published in Polish.)

London, Kurt. ([1936] 1970). *Film Music.* New York: Arno Press.

Lotman, Jurij. (1979). "The Origin of Plot in the Light of Typology," trans. Julian Graffy, *Poetics Today* 1, 1–2, pp. 161–84.

Lyons, Len. (1980). *The 101 Best Jazz Albums: A History of Jazz on Records.* New York: William Morrow, pp. 327–61.

MacCabe, Colin (Ed.). (1986). *High Theory/Low Culture: Analysing Popular Television and Film.* New York: St. Martin's Press.

Maio, Kathi. (1991). "Women Who Murder for the Man," *Ms.* 11, 3 (November-December), pp. 82–84.

Manuel, Peter. (1988). *Popular Musics of the Non-Western World: An Introductory Survey.* New York and Oxford: Oxford University Press.

Manvell, Roger and John Huntley. (1975). *The Technique of Film Music.* London, 1957. New York: Hastings House.

Marker, Chris. (1997). *The Rest Is Silent.* Essay accompanying installation at Werner Art Center.

Marks, Martin. (1997). *Music and the Silent Film: Contexts and Case Studies, 1895–1924.* New York and Oxford: Oxford University Press.

Martin, Mick and Marsha Porter. (1991). *Video Movie Guide 1992.* New York: Ballantine Books.

McClary, Susan. (1986). "A Musical Dialectic from the Enlightenment: Mozart's Piano Concerto in G Major, K. 453, Movement 2," *Cultural Critique* 4, pp. 129–70.

———. (1991). *Feminine Endings: Music, Gender, and Sexuality.* Minneapolis: University of Minnesota Press.

Melville, Stephen W. (1986). *Philosophy beside Itself: On Deconstruction and Modernism.* Minneapolis: University of Minnesota Press.

Mermelstein, David. (1997). "In Hollywood, Discord on What Makes Music," *New York Times,* Sunday, November 2, pp. AR 17, AR 30.

Metz, Christian. (1982). *The Imaginary Signifier: Psychoanalysis and the Cinema,* trans. Celia Britton et al. Bloomington: Indiana University Press.

Meyer, Leonard B. (1956). *Emotion and Meaning in Music.* Chicago: University of Chicago Press.

Middleton, Richard. (1990). *Studying Popular Music.* Milton Keynes (UK), and Philadelphia: Open University Press.

Modleski, Tania (Ed.). (1986). *Studies in Entertainment: Critical Approaches to Mass Culture.* Bloomington and Indianapolis: Indiana University Press.

———. (1991). *Feminism without Women.* New York: Routledge.

Mowitt, John. (1992). *Text: The Genealogy of an Antidisciplinary Object.* Durham, NC: Duke University Press.

Mulvey, Laura. (1989). "Visual Pleasure and Narrative Cinema," in *Visual*

and Other Pleasures. Bloomington and Indianapolis: Indiana University
  Press, pp. 14–26.

Nattiez, Jean-Jacques. (1975). *Fondements d'une sémiologie de la musique.* Paris:
  Union Générale d'Éditions.

Negus, Keith. (1996). *Popular Music in Theory: An Introduction.* Hanover, NH:
  Wesleyan University Press/University Press of New England.

Peirce, Charles Sanders. (1991). *Peirce on Signs.* Chapel Hill: University of
  North Carolina Press.

Rapee, Erno. (1925). *Erno Rapee's Encyclopedia of Music for Pictures.* New York:
  Belwin. (Reprinted 1970. New York: Arno Press.)

Rogin, Michael. (1987). *"Ronald Reagan," the Movie: And Other Episodes in
  Political Demonology.* Berkeley: University of California Press.

Rony, Fatimah Tobing. (1997). *The Third Eye: Race, Cinema, and Ethnographic
  Spectacle.* Durham, NC: Duke University Press.

Rosen, Marjorie. (1973). *Popcorn Venus: Women, Movies, and the American Dream.*
  New York: Avon Books.

Rosolato, Guy, "La voix: Entre corps et langage," *Revue française de
  psychanalyse* 37, 1, pp. 75–94.

Rule, Jane. (1986). *Desert of the Heart.* Tallahasee, FL: Naiad Press.

Sabaneev, Leonid. (1935). *Music for the Films: A Handbook for Composers and
  Conductors,* trans. S. W. Pring. London: Sir Isaac Pitman & Sons.

Saussure, Ferdinand de. (1959). *Course in General Linguistics.* New York:
  Philosophical Library.

Schudson, Michael. (1986). *What Time Means in a News Story.* New York:
  Gannett Center for Media Studies.

Schwarz, David. (1997a). "Listening Subjects: Semiotics, Psychoanalysis,
  and the Music of John Adams and Steve Reich," in David Schwarz,
  Anahid Kassabian, and Lawrence Siegel (Eds.), *Keeping Score: Music,
  Disciplinarity, Culture.* Charlottesville: University Press of Virginia.
  (Reprinted from *Perspectives on New Music,* 1993.)

———. (1997b). *Listening Subjects: Music, Psychoanalysis, Culture.* Durham, NC:
  Duke University Press.

Schwarz, David, Anahid Kassabian, and Lawrence Siegel (Eds.). (1997).
  Keeping Score: Music, Disciplinarity, Culture. Charlottesville: University Press
  of Virginia.

Screen. (1990). "Editorial," 31, 1, pp. 1–5.

Seiter, Ellen. (1990). Contribution to *Camera Obscura* 20–21 (special issue on
  "The Spectatrix"), pp. 282–84.

Selected Sounds Recorded Music Library. (n.d.). Hamburg: Selected Sound
  Musikverlag GMBH & CO KG.

Shepherd, John. (1987). "Music and Male Hegemony," in Richard Leppert
  and Susan McClary (Eds.), *Music and Society: The Politics of Composition,
  Performance, and Reception.* New York: Cambridge University Press,
  pp. 151–72.

———. (1993). "Popular Music: Challenges to Musicology," in *Stanford
  Humanities Review* 3, 2.

Showalter, Elaine. (1985). *The Female Malady: Women, Madness, and English
  Culture 1830–1980.* New York: Penguin.

Shumway, David. (1999). "Rock and Roll Soundtracks and the
  Production of Nostalgia," *Cinema Journal* 38, 2, pp. 36–51.

Silverman, Kaja. (1988). *The Acoustic Mirror: The Female Voice in Psychoanalysis
  and Cinema.* Bloomington: Indiana University Press.

———. (1992). *Male Subjectivity at the Margins.* New York and London:
  Routledge.

———. (1996). *The Threshold of the Visible World.* New York and London:
  Routledge.

Smith, Jeff. (1998). *The Sounds of Commerce: Marketing Popular Film Music.* New
  York: Columbia University Press.

Sobchack, Vivian. (1986). "Child/Alien/Father: Patriarchal Crisis and
  Generic Exchange," *Camera Obscura* 15, pp. 7–34.

Solie, Ruth (Ed.). (1993). *Musicology and Difference.* Berkeley: University of
  California Press.

Stockfelt, Ola. (1997). "Adequate Modes of Listening," trans. A. Kassabian
  and L. G. Svendsen, in *Keeping Score: Music, Disciplinarity, Culture.*
  Charlottesville: University Press of Virginia.

Stravinsky, Igor. (1936). *Chronicle of My Life.* London: Gollancz.

Swiss, Thom, John Sloop, and Andrew Herman (Eds). (1998). *Mapping the
  Beat: Popular Music and Contemporary Theory.* Malden, MA: Blackwell.

Tagg, Philip. (n.d.). "Nature as a Musical Mood Category," International
  Association for the Study of Popular Music Working Papers, #P8026.

———. (1979). *Kojak—50 Seconds of Television Music: Toward the Analysis of
  Affect in Popular Music.* Göteborg, Sweden: Skrifter från
  Musikvetenskapliga Institutionen, No. 2.

———. (1990a), "An Anthropology of Stereotypes in TV Music?" in
  Svensk tidskrift för musikforskning, 1989, pp.19–42.

———. (1990b). " 'Universal' Music and the Case of Death," in R. Pozzi

(Ed.), *La Musica Come Linguaggio Universale: Genesi e Storia di un'Idea.* Florence: Leo S. Olschki Editore.

Tagg, Philip and Robert Clarida. (n.d.). *Ten Little Title Tunes.* Liverpool: Institute for Popular Music Research Report.

Taussig, Michael. (1989). "Dada and Homesickness," *Stanford Humanities Review* 1, 1, pp. 44–81.

Thomas, Tony. (1973). *Music for the Movies.* South Brunswick and New York: A. S. Barnes.

Tomlinson, Gary. (1993). *Music in Renaissance Magic: Toward a Historiography of Others.* Chicago: University of Chicago Press.

Vasconcelos, Jose. ([1925] 1979). *La Raza Cosmica = The Cosmic Race: A Bilingual Edition,* introduction and notes by Didier T. Jaen. Los Angeles: Department of Chicano Studies, California State University, Los Angeles. (Originally published in Spanish.)

Walser, Robert. (1995). "Rhythm, Rhyme, and Rhetoric in the Music of Public Enemy," *Ethnomusicology* 39, 2 (Spring/Summer 1995), pp. 193–217.

Willis, Sharon. (1997). *High Contrast: Race and Gender in Contemporary Hollywood Films.* Raleigh, NC: Duke University Press.

Winkler, Peter. (1997). "Writing Ghost Notes: The Poetics and Politics of Transcription," in David Schwarz, Anahid Kassabian, and Lawrence Siegel (Eds.), *Keeping Score: Music, Disciplinarity, Culture.* Charlottesville: University Press of Virginia.

Videos Cited

10 (1979, USA), directed by Blake Edwards, music by Henry Mancini. Burbank, CA: Warner Home Video.

Above the Law (1988, USA), directed by Andrew Davis, music by David Frank. Burbank, CA: Warner Home Video.

American Graffiti (1973, USA), directed by George Lucas, compiled score. Universal City, CA: MCA/Universal Home Video.

American Me (1992, USA), directed by Edward James Olmos, music by Dennis Lambert. Universal City, CA: MCA/Universal Home Video.

An American Tail (1986, USA), directed by Don Bluth, music by James Horner and Barry Mann II. Universal City, CA: Universal Studios.

Apocalypse Now (1979, USA), directed by Francis Ford Coppola, music by Carmine Coppola. Los Angeles: Paramount Home Video.

Armageddon (1998, USA), directed by Michael Bay, music by Trevor Rabin and Harry Gregson-Williams. Burbank, CA: Touchstone Video.

Back to the Future (1985, USA), directed by Robert Zemeckis, music by Alan Silvestri. Universal City, CA: MCA/Universal Home Video.

Bagdad Cafe (1988, West Germany), directed by Percy Adlon, music by Bob Telson. Los Angeles: Virgin Vision.

The Big Chill (1983, USA), directed by Lawrence Kasdan, compiled score. Culver City, CA: Columbia Tristar Home Video.

The Birth of a Nation (1915, USA), directed by D. W. Griffith. Sandy Hook, CT: Video Images (Allied Arts Entertainment).

Blackboard Jungle (1955, USA), directed by Richard Brooks. Culver City, CA: MGM/UA Studios.

Blaze (1989, USA), directed by Ron Shelton, music by Bennie Wallace. Burbank, CA: Buena Vista Home Video.

Bonnie and Clyde (1967, USA), directed by Arthur Penn, music by Charles Strouse, "Foggy Mountain Breakdown" by Flatt and Scruggs. Burbank, CA: Warner Home Video.

Born on the Fourth of July (1989, USA), directed by Oliver Stone, music by John Williams. Universal City, CA: MCA/Universal Home Video.

Boyz N the Hood (1991, USA), directed by John Singleton, music by Stanley Clarke. Culver City, CA: Columbia Tristar Home Video.

Braveheart (1995, USA), directed by Mel Gibson, music by James Horner. Hollywood, CA: Paramount Studios.

Captain Blood (1935, USA), directed by Michael Curtiz, music by Erich Wolfgang Korngold. Culver City, CA: MGM/UA Studios.

Close Encounters of the Third Kind (1977, USA), directed by Steven Spielberg, music by John Williams. Culver City, CA: Columbia Tristar Home Video.

Corrina, Corrina (1994, USA), directed by Jessie Nelson, music by Thomas Newman and Rick Cox. Los Angeles: New Line Home Video.

Cruel Intentions (1999, USA), directed by Roger Kumble, music by Edward Shearmur. Culver City, CA: Columbia Tristar Home Video.

Dances with Wolves (1990, USA), directed by Kevin Costner, music by John Barry. Los Angeles: Orion Home Video.

Dangerous Liaisons (1988, USA), directed by Stephen Frears, music by George Fenton. Burbank, CA: Warner Home Video.

Dangerous Minds (1995, USA), directed by John N. Smith, music by Wendy and Lisa. Burbank, CA: Buena Vista Home Video.

Day of Wrath (*Vredens Dag*) (1943, Denmark), directed by Carl Theodor Dreyer, music by Poul Schierbeck. Fort Wayne, IN: Hen's Tooth Video.

Dead Again (1991, USA), directed by Kenneth Branagh, music by Patrick Doyle. Los Angeles: Paramount Home Video.

Death in Venice (*Morte a Venezia*) (1971, Italy), directed by Luchino Visconti, music by Gustav Mahler. Burbank, CA: Warner Home Video.

Desert Hearts (1985, USA), directed by Donna Deitch, compiled score. Van Nuys, CA: Vestron Video.

Dirty Dancing (1987, USA), directed by Emile Ardolino, music by John Morris. Van Nuys, CA: Vestron Video.

The Dresser (1983, UK), directed by Peter Yates, music by James Horner. Culver City, CA: Columbia Tristar Home Video.

Easy Rider (1969, US), directed by Dennis Hopper, compiled score (including songs by Steppenwolf, The Jimi Hendrix Experience, etc.), "Ballad

of Easy Rider" written and performed by Roger McGuinn. Culver
　City, CA: Columbia Tristar Studios.

The Empire Strikes Back (1980, USA), directed by Irvin Kershner, music by
　John Williams. Los Angeles: Fox Video.

Flashdance (1983, USA), directed by Adrian Lyne, music by Dennis
　Matkosky, Giorgio Moroder, and Michael Sembello. Hollywood, CA:
　Paramount Studios.

For the Boys (1991, USA), directed by Mark Rydell, music by Dave Grusin.
　Los Angeles: Fox Video.

The French Connection (1971, USA), directed by William Friedkin, music by
　Don Ellis. Beverly Hills, CA: CBS/Fox Video.

Good Morning, Vietnam (1987, USA), directed by Barry Levinson, music by
　Alex North. Burbank, CA: Buena Vista Home Video.

The Graduate (1967, USA), directed by Mike Nichols, music by Dave Grusin,
　songs by Paul Simon. New York: Polygram Video.

The Hunt for Red October (1990, USA), directed by John McTiernan, music by
　Basil Poledouris. Los Angeles: Paramount Home Video.

I Like It Like That (1994, USA), directed by Darnell Martin, music by Sergio
　George. Culver City, CA: Columbia Tristar Home Video.

Indiana Jones and the Temple of Doom (1984, USA), directed by Steven Spielberg,
　music by John Williams. Los Angeles: Paramount Home Video.

Jaws (1975, USA), directed by Steven Spielberg, music by John Williams.
　Universal City, CA: MCA/Universal Home Video.

Jules et Jim (1962, France), directed by François Truffaut, music by Georges
　Delerue. Beverly Hills, CA: CBS/Fox Video.

Laura (1944, USA), directed by Otto Preminger, music by David Raksin.
　Beverly Hills, CA: Twentieth Century–Fox Film Corp.

Lean on Me (1989, USA), directed by John G. Avildsen, music by Bill Conti.
　Burbank, CA: Warner Studios.

Lethal Weapon (1987, USA), directed by Richard Donner, music by Michael
　Kamen and Eric Clapton. Burbank, CA: Warner Home Video.

Lethal Weapon 2 (1989, USA), directed by Richard Donner, music by
　Michael Kamen, Eric Clapton, and David Sanborn. Burbank, CA:
　Warner Home Video.

Lethal Weapon 3 (1992, USA), directed by Richard Donner, music by
　Michael Kamen, Eric Clapton, and David Sanborn. Burbank, CA:
　Warner Home Video.

Malcolm X (1992, USA), directed by Spike Lee, music by Terence
   Blanchard. Burbank, CA: Warner Home Video.

Mallrats (1995, USA), directed by Kevin Smith, music by Ira Newborn.
   Universal City, CA: MCA/Universal Home Video.

The Mask of Zorro (1998, USA), directed by Martin Campbell, music by
   James Horner. Culver City, CA: Columbia/Tristar Studios.

Mi Familia/My Family (1994, USA), directed by Gregory Nava, music by
   Pepe Avila and Mark McKenzie. Los Angeles: New Line Home Video.

Mi Vida Loca (1994, USA), directed by Allison Anders, music by John
   Taylor. New York: HBO Home Video.

Miami Vice (1984, USA), directed by Thomas Carter, music by Jan
   Hammer. Universal City, CA: MCA/Universal Home Video.

Mildred Pierce (1945, USA), directed by Michael Curtiz, music by Max
   Steiner. Beverly Hills, CA: CBS/Fox Video.

Mississippi Masala (1992, USA), directed by Mira Nair, music by L.
   Subramaniam. Culver City, CA: Columbia Tristar Home Video.

Moonstruck (1987, USA), directed by Norman Jewison, music by Dick
   Hyman, *La Bohème* by Giacomo Puccini. Los Angeles: MGM/UA Home
   Video.

Ordinary People (1980, USA), directed by Robert Redford, music by Marvin
   Hamlisch. Los Angeles: Paramount Home Video.

Philadelphia (1993, USA), directed by Jonathan Demme, music by Howard
   Shore, Bruce Springsteen, Neil Young. Culver City, CA:
   Columbia/Tristar Studios.

Rebecca (1940, USA), directed by Alfred Hitchcock, music by Franz
   Waxman. Troy, MI: Anchor Bay Entertainment.

Rebel Without a Cause (1955, USA), directed by Nicholas Ray, music by
   Leonard Rosenman. Burbank, CA: Warner Home Video.

Return of the Jedi (1983, USA), directed by Richard Marquand, music by
   John Williams. Beverly Hills, CA: CBS/Fox Video.

Romeo and Juliet (1968, Italy), directed by Franco Zeffirelli, music by Nino
   Rota. Los Angeles: Paramount Home Video

Saturday Night Fever (1977, USA), directed by John Badham, music by David
   Shire. Los Angeles: Paramount Home Video.

Sleeping with the Enemy (1991, USA), directed by Joseph Ruben, music by
   Jerry Goldsmith. Los Angeles: Twentieth Century–Fox Video.

Stand and Deliver (1987, USA), directed by Ramón Menéndez, music by
   Craig Safan. Burbank, CA: Warner Studios.

Star Trek: Deep Space Nine (USA). Los Angeles: Paramount Home Video.

Star Wars (1977, USA), directed by George Lucas, music by John Williams. Beverly Hills, CA: CBS/Fox Video.

The Sting (1973, USA), directed by George Roy Hill, music by Marvin Hamlisch. Universal City, CA: MCA/Universal Home Video.

A Streetcar Named Desire (1951, USA), directed by Elia Kazan, music by Alex North. Beverly Hills, CA: CBS/Fox Video.

The Substitute (1996, USA), directed by Robert Mandel, music by Gary Chang. Van Nuys, CA: Live Home Video.

Thelma and Louise (1991, USA), directed by Ridley Scott, music by Hans Zimmer. Santa Monica, CA: MGM/UA Home Video.

Tomorrow Never Dies (1997, UK/USA), directed by Roger Spottiswoode, music by David Arnold II, Don Black, and Sheryl Crow. Santa Monica, CA: MGM/UA Home Video.

Total Recall (1990, USA), directed by Paul Verhoeven, music by Jerry Goldsmith. Van Nuys, CA: Live Home Video.

Waiting to Exhale (1995, USA), directed by Forest Whitaker, music by Babyface. Beverly Hills, CA: Twentieth Century Fox–Film Corp.

A Woman Under the Influence (1974, USA), directed by John Cassavetes, music by Bo Harwood. Chicago, IL: Facets Multimedia (Pioneer Video).

Young Sherlock Holmes (1985, USA), directed by Barry Levinson, music by Bruce Broughton. Los Angeles: Paramount Home Video.

Notes

Prologue

1. It was enormously difficult to find a name for theoretical film-goers that avoided the visuality of "spectator" and also articulated some degree of agency in that space. The obvious counterpart to "spectator"— "auditor"—simply reverses the hierarchy of vision over sound, and therefore doesn't work to mark theoretical filmgoers either. Following Bordwell and Thompson (1993) and Christian Metz (1982), I chose "perceiver" for this purpose, because despite its etymology it does not privilege one sense over others, and because it is slightly more active in tone than "spectator" or "auditor."
2. *Indiana Jones and the Temple of Doom* (ch. 4), *The Hunt for Red October* (ch. 4), and *The Mask of Zorro* (epilogue), respectively.
3. See Jeff Smith's *The Sounds of Commerce* for an important analysis of pop scores and their market functions.
4. Many film scholars work on films from other nations, particularly Germany, France, Italy, Japan, and India, and many more work on avant-garde and experimental filmmakers. There is also an important tradition of documentary film scholarship. None of this, however, undercuts the argument that film studies is organized around Hollywood from 1900 to 1950: genre studies, *auteur* theory, semiotics, and psychoanalytic film theory and others draw most heavily on that segment of film history.
5. Goldmark made these comments at the April 1999 Iowa University Cinema and Popular Song conference.
6. See the discussions of "corporeality in music" in Middleton (1990) and of the problem of essentialism in the study of music in Shepherd (1993).

7. It is worth noting that the only tradition within music studies that concerns itself with meaning is ethnomusicology, which specifically studies music outside the western art tradition.

8. See, for some examples, McClary and Leppert 1987; Kramer 1990; McClary 1991; Bergeron and Bohlman 1992; Tomlinson 1993; Solie 1993; Brett, Wood, and Thomas 1994; Brackett 1995; Schwarz, Kassabian, and Siegel 1997; Swiss, Sloop, and Herman 1997.

Chapter 1

1. Prices and price structures for music library uses vary widely. Some companies charge one flat fee for "eternal" permission, while others charge needle-drop (per use) fees, and still others some combination of the two. Some companies sell one or two CD series, others entire libraries. In November 1992, one company, Network, charged $3,000 per year for unlimited use of a library of 100 CDs with seven to nine themes each; Magic Tracks charged $79.95 per twelve-theme CD for permanent permission; Music Annex in San Francisco charged needle-drop rates from $100–300 per theme, depending on the use, plus studio time for selecting the theme.

2. For information on the publication of this study, see Tagg's home page, www.liv.ac.uk/IPM/tagg/articles/tvanthro.htm.

3. This study was as "uncoached" as possible—respondents were simply asked to write down any associations, what they saw on their "minds' screens," in response to the music they heard. The respondents crossed age and gender lines, although most were between the ages of seventeen and twenty-five; most of the six hundred-plus respondents were Swedish, although approximately thirty were South American. They were self-selected to the extent that they were attending lectures on film music, although the lectures were given in many different contexts and they were by no means mainly people with sustained interest in film, music, or film music.

4. The choice of a word to describe a group of musical events with similar intra- and extramusical features is rather complicated. Here, "musical genre" is used for a set of intramusical features (on-beat simple rhythmic patterns, simple three-chord harmonic patterns, "coarse," "scratchy" vocal production, little or no varia-

tion in dynamics or tempo, high volume, etc.) *and* extramusical associations (spiked hair of various unnatural colors, leather and studded clothing, safety pins, the pogo, cocaine, unemployment, alienation, etc.) that combine to give meaning to a name like "punk." This definition is from Franco Fabbri, who defines musical genre as "a set of musical events (real or possible) whose course is governed by a set of socially accepted rules" (1982: 52).

5. In other words, while it may be so that members of all cultures acquire competence in music, it does not follow that members of all cultures acquire competence in the same music, nor that competence in one music is transferable to others. Tagg (1990b) describes the responses of Swedes concerned with issues of immigrant culture to death-related music from African, Asian, and Near and Middle Eastern cultures. Not one response included any words like "death," "funeral," or "wake," and several even included associations such as "wedding," "birth," "joy," and "street parade." Quite obviously, even though both death and music may be universal human phenomena, any connections between the two are culturally specific.

6. Not all music scholars agree. Frith, Grossberg, and Shepherd have each argued, throughout their works, positions that hear music nonsemiotically.

7. Thanks to Greg Sandow for these calculations.

8. Dominant ideologies of music make it difficult to recognize music as a set of cultural conventions that contains repeatable and often repeated material. This recognition would undercut several widely circulating discourses, such as the notion that musics produced by digital sampling (rap, Negativland, Art of Noise) are less original than composed musics.

9. The musical examples in this study were chosen precisely because they are "classical Hollywood practice." The themes were: "Dream of Olwen," "Monty Python," "The Virginian," "Romeo and Juliet," "Emmerdale Farm," "Sayonara," "Sportsnight," "Streetcar Named Desire," "Miami Vice," and "Owed to 'g'" (a Deep Purple song that many listeners identified neither as film nor television music). Unfortunately, Tagg and Clarida did not collect information on their respondents, so there is no way to know if their responses differed along gender or other lines.

10. Tables 1 to 4 in Appendix B contain the data I compiled from Tagg and Clarida's results.
11. For a concise explanation of the public/private split, see Jaggar 1989: 143–48.

Chapter 2

1. I have located relatively few books outside of English as well (it is, of course, likely that there is more work than I have found). For two important examples of film music scholarship not yet translated into English, see Lissa 1965 and Lacombe and Roclé 1979.
2. This model is vastly more useful in the diagram form in which it appears on p. 47 of Johnson's text.
3. For critiques of this model, see Gorbman 1987: 15, 145; Gallez 1970; Eisler and Adorno 1947: 70; and Kalinak 1992: 24–30.
4. Although Eisler appears as the sole author on the original English edition, which appeared first, it is generally accepted that Adorno was coauthor of the text, as he is credited on the German edition. In a recent reprinting of the book, he is listed as the first author.
5. Even "source scoring" might not account for all of the film music uses that are neither dramatic scoring nor source music. Gorbman's example from *Blackmail*, wherein a woman "hears" a previously diegetic piano theme (26), does not literally fit Hagen's definition of source scoring.
6. One clear reason for hearing this sequence differently could be a difference in listening habits. For a listener trained to hear themes and motifs in music, the recurrence of earlier themes would be much more noticeable than for a listener who did not attend to musical materials so consciously.
7. It is interesting to note that leitmotiv is not the only practice film music has taken from Wagner; in fact, many of film music's "codes" are based on German late Romanticism. For an extended analysis of the relationship between film music and Romanticism, see Flinn 1992.
8. I have chosen to retain Brecht's term in the original German because I believe that it has lost its focus in common usage. "Alienation-effect" or "distanciation-effect"—the standard translations—have come to mean something like "a technique that encourages rational critical distance." The term would better be translated as

"anti-identification" or "anti-suture effect." As Martin Esslin describes: "Moreover, the audience must be *discouraged* from losing its critical detachment by *identification* with one or more characters: the opposite of identification is the maintenance of a separate existence by being kept apart, alien, strange...That is the meaning of the famous 'Verfremdungseffekt', a term which has never been successfully rendered in English" (p. 115).

Chapter 3

1. This is not to say that *only* films with strong female characters use pop scores, or that *all* films with strong female characters use pop scores, but rather that a significant number of films with strong female characters do. One important set of counterexamples is action-adventure or sci-fi-adventure films, like *The Abyss* or the *Alien* films, which use Romantic classical scores.

2. Kathi Maio's "Women Who Murder for the Man" (*Ms.*, December 1991: 82–84) quotes a smattering of verbally violent responses from male reviewers. For example, Ralph Novak said in *People*: "Any movie that went as far out of its way to trash women as this female chauvinist sow of a film does to trash men would be universally, and justifiably, condemned." Maio suggests in response that "slasher films and so-called thrillers constitute a continual stream of female blood" and argues that safe women killers, like Julia Roberts's character in *Sleeping with the Enemy*, kill to reinforce patriarchy and heterosexuality rather than killing to evade or disrupt it as Thelma and Louise do. (Lisa Hogeland first showed me the Thelma and Louise button, and I am both grateful and jealous.)

3. It would be an important project to try to sort out the relationship between the economics of compiled scores (i.e., what they cost in editing and mixing labor compared to the costs of composing, orchestrating, performing, editing, and mixing composed scores, what royalties cost for each song and each soundtrack as a whole versus what they bring in in soundtrack sales and free advertising through radio play) and the way they operate in lived culture. For a discussion of the economics and more, see Smith 1998.

4. Gay and lesbian country music audiences have remade the meanings of the genre for their own purposes in ways that would be well worth studying.

5.   It is unclear how this might affect the traditional heterosexual male fantasy of watching women make love to each other. Based on the camera work and lack of score, I don't think this sequence is addressed to such a voyeuristic fantasy, but it doesn't seem to preclude it either.

6.   Jazz in general and here Ella Fitzgerald also mark a musical discourse about race and class; in this sense, "I Wished on the Moon" is an odd choice for a film that so assiduously denies the presence of nonwhite peoples in Nevada.

7.   Frith and McRobbie briefly discuss Tammy Wynette in "Rock and Sexuality." They suggest that the sexism of the lyrics Wynette sings is undercut by the quality of her voice: "'Sometimes it's hard to be a woman,' Tammy Wynette begins, and you can hear that it's hard and you can hear that Tammy Wynette knows why—her voice is a collective one" (1990: 385). It would be interesting to pursue an inquiry into what makes a voice collective in this sense. One answer might be timbre, on which see Shepherd 1987, and Brackett 1996. Wynette also signifies as a star with a history of multiple stormy marriages, who sang "D-I-V-O-R-C-E," and who here is singing a country version of an Elvis rock song.

8.   Sharon Willis makes an excellent argument that the standard of realism assumes a troubling mimetic model of identification. "Such a drive," she says, "to regulate the film according to plausibility suggests that the desire for it to work as a feminist parable or prescription also serves an agenda of containment. For this drive depends on forgetting that the film's spectacle is made of the play between plausibility and fantasy, a play organized around the figure of a body, but a body catapulting across the landscape in a car, indissociable from motion, from the drive forward into loss" (1997: 104).

Chapter 4

1.   It is interesting to note that many fusion stars who come to mind are white but ethnically marked in some way, unlike, for instance, their rock superstar counterparts.

2.   Willis discusses the homoerotics of the relationship between Riggs and Murtaugh and its dependence on race (1997: 27–59).

3. Note the lack of harmonic motion. There is relatively little construction of desire here, no real drive to resolution; rather, the music produces a sense of timelessness.
4. Her work remains both commonly read and in the modern literary canon of Scandinavia, and at least three women have made albums of songs based on her poetry. The full text of the poem, in my translation, appears in Appendix C.
5. Willis points out how frequently the *Lethal Weapon* films recognize their own homoerotic subtext:

> *Lethal Weapon 2* exhibits a particularly—and jocularly—anxious fascination with its own homoerotic subtext, expressed in Riggs's jokes on two occasions. When his partner, Roger Murtaugh (Danny Glover), finds himself sitting on a toilet that is wired with explosives, Riggs loyally remains with his partner for the controlled detonation that ensues. The two end up in a sexually suggestive pose, with Riggs on his back and Murtaugh on top of him. Riggs smirkingly suggests that they get out of this embrace, as he wouldn't "want anyone to find us like this." At the film's end, we find Murtaugh holding the wounded Riggs in his lap, as they wait for the police to arrive. Riggs quips "Give us a kiss before they get here." Such wit here seems designed to diffuse and contain the overtly homoerotic charge these scenes produce—to offer and then withdraw the lure of homoeroticism. (1997: 28–29)

Chapter 5

1. Wendy Melvoin and Lisa Coleman, formerly of Prince's back-up group.
2. For a discussion of pedagogy films, see Giroux 1993.
3. An interesting case might be made that rap, by its very musical structures, wards off assimilating identifications. Rob Walser's analysis (1995) of polyrhythms in "Fight the Power" by Public Enemy, for example, does not address identification processes but could lead in such a direction.
4. Interestingly, *The Perez Family* bombed at the box office. One explanation for its difficulties was the concurrent release of *My Family/Mi Familia*, which, while it also didn't last in theaters, was consistently

reviewed favorably and in direct competition with *The Perez Family.* Nair's next project, *Kama Sutra,* focused on female sexuality and was pointedly independent in content and distribution.

5.   The setting looks more like a railroad car than a restaurant, and Willie Ben's uniform looks like a porter's. Overall, the sequence makes evocative references to all the black men in the South who worked as porters on trains throughout the first half of the twentieth century and their groundbreaking 1950s labor struggles.

6.   At one point relatively early in the film, Kanti, one of the Indian motel owners, decides to persuade Demetrius not to sue because of the crash. He takes a cup of tea to Demetrius and Tyrone as they are cleaning the carpets in his motel, and spouts opportunistic platitudes like "United we stand, divided we fall" and "All of us people of color have got to stick together." Throughout the film, Tyrone and Demetrius ridicule the bankruptcy of this mercenary alliance-building tactic. But in the final sequence, is there a real difference between Kanti's rhetoric and the film's reliance on African music to wash away the differences between Demetrius's experiences and Mina's? And if the history of Indian nationals in Uganda had not been erased in the opening sequences, would the connection between Mina and Demetrius remain so happily untroubled?

Epilogue

1.   For example, see Henry Giroux's contribution to *Film Theory Goes to the Movies,* in which he discusses pedagogy films along these lines.

2.   It is difficult to count the occurrences of the theme. I have chosen not to count each of the numerous times the theme appears in a fight sequence, for instance. I have counted the first appearance in the scene, which generally identifies Zorro's presence before the fighting breaks out, and then all of the occurrences during the fighting as one. The point of counting is, in any case, not so much to quantify precisely as to get a sense of proportions.

Index

Verdi, 94

Verfremdungseffekt, 59

W

Wagner, Richard, 50

Waiting to Exhale, 4

Walser, Rob, 179n. 3

Washington, Denzel, 123–25

Whitley, Chris, 84

Williams, John, 3, 47, 51, 92, 104

Williams, Robin, 86

Willis, Sharon, 8, 178nn. 2, 179n. 5; *High Contrast,* 86

Winkler, Peter, 21

Woman Under the Influence, A, 50

women, 4, 30, 33–36, 61–90, 103; and romance, 35–36; of color, 123

Wynette, Tammy, 81, 82, 178n. 7.

Y

Young Sherlock Holmes, 51

Z

Zawinul, Josef, 100

Zimmer, Hans, 3